THE STON...

GL
BOU...

CW01460788

EDITED BY J.S. WATSON

**Copyright © Stone Country Press 2022**

1st edition, published 2022 by Stone Country Press Ltd.

The right of the editors to be identified as the authors of this work has been asserted in accordance with the Copyright, Designs and Patents Act, 1988.

A CIP catalogue record for this book is available from the British Library.

Designed by Stone Country

Printed and bound by Severn

ISBN 978-0-992887-64-3

A CIP catalogue record for this book is available from the British Library.

www.stonecountrypress.co.uk

Frontispiece photo of Lucy Ross bouldering at Craigmaddie © Roxanna Barry

**DISCLAIMER**
Rock climbing can be a dangerous sport that can lead to serious risk and injury. You should not undertake the routes described in this guide without proper experience, training or equipment. By using this guide, you acknowledge that the information therein may be out of date or inaccurate, and you agree that the publisher cannot be held liable for any damage or injury that may be caused when climbing the routes in this guide. Climbers must accept responsibility for judging a route before climbing it. The contents of this guide have been checked to be as accurately described as possible at the date of publication. The publisher cannot be held responsible for any omissions or mistakes, nor liable for any personal or third party injuries. It is recommended that climbers obtain suitable insurance and assume all responsibility for their climbing.

# CONTENTS

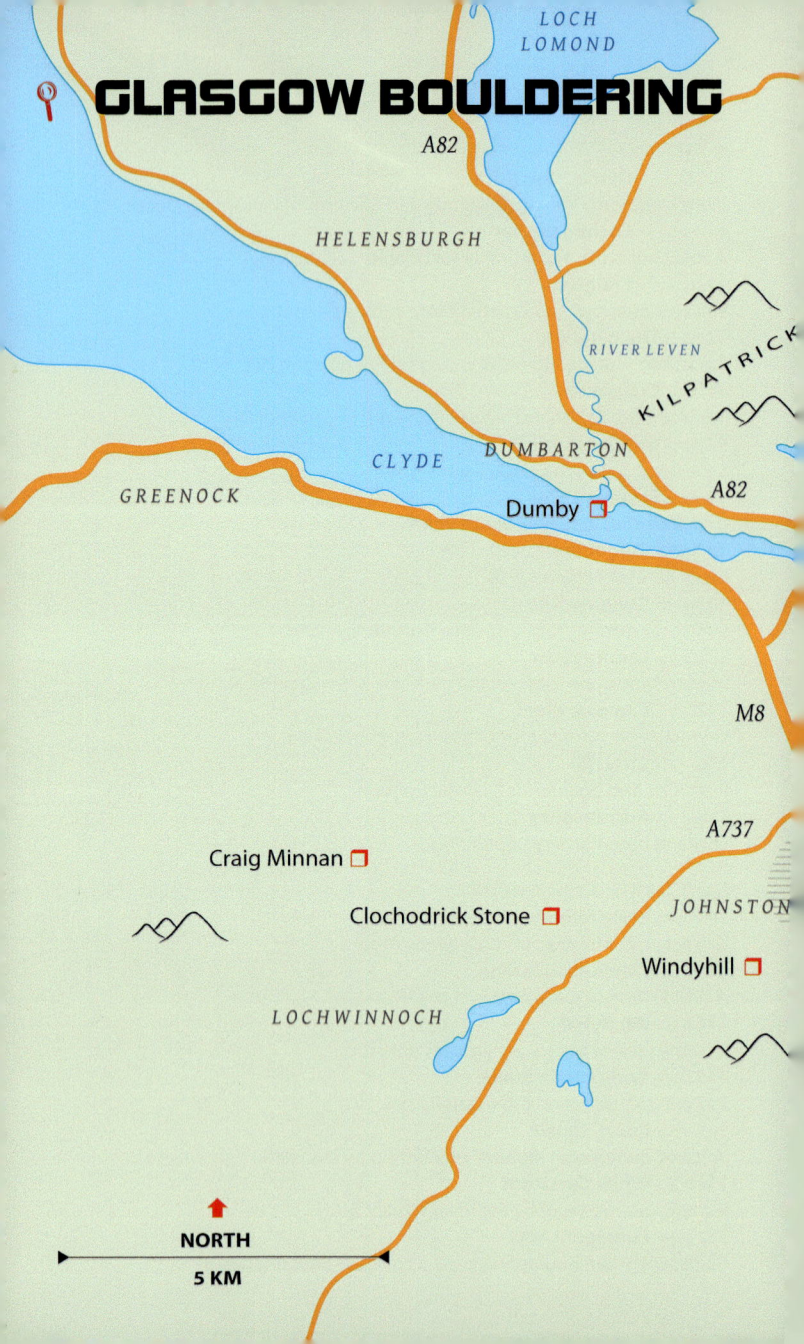

# GLASGOW BOULDERING

LOCH LOMOND

A82

HELENSBURGH

KILPATRICK

RIVER LEVEN

DUMBARTON

CLYDE

GREENOCK

Dumby

A82

M8

A737

Craig Minnan

Clochodrick Stone

JOHNSTON

Windyhill

LOCHWINNOCH

NORTH

5 KM

Stronend Bloc ☐

A809

☐ Garloch Hill

CAMPSIE FELLS

STRATHBLANE

HILLS

☐ The Whangie

☐ Campsie Blocs

☐ Lennoxtown

☐ Craigmore

☐ Craigmaddie

Craigton ☐

Auchinstarry ☐

☐ Cochno Stones

A81

KIRKINTILLOCH

MILNGAVIE

BEARSDEN

M80

A82

GLASGOW

M8

✈

PAISLEY

Cuningar Loop ☐

M74

☐ Andromeda Stane

☐ Court Knowe

RIVER CLYDE

BUSBY

WHITE CART

HAMILTON

M77

EAST KILBRIDE

# GLASGOW BOULDERING: A BRIEF HISTORY

## RAILWAY WALLS AND BRIDGES

They are rarely climbed these days, but the only source of climbing training in the early-to-late part of the twentieth century were the sandstone railway walls and bridge buttresses, such as the blond sandstone walls opposite the SECC on the Clydeside Expressway, the red sandstone South Street walls, or the Kelvinbridge walls on the north bank of the River Kelvin on Great Western Road, and on a canal flyover at Lock 27 on the Forth and Clyde canal at Netherton. Many other sandstone walls can be found round the city. These 'buildering' walls always allowed good stamina training, as they had 'pinch-pockets' in the centre of the sandstone blocks from the iron clamps used to lift them, so they always provided finger-strengthening holes just like a modern fingerboard. Some of the walls, such as the Clydeside Expressway buttress, provided bold solos to their tops and illegal escapes along the tracks! Of course, all this is forbidden now due to safety legislation, though the walls are still accessible. These sandstone walls used to be much more frequented before the first indoor walls were built and Glasgow saw its first indoor climbing centres. The most famous of these indoor walls was the resin wall of the Kelvin Hall Sports Centre (opposite the Kelvingrove Museum), which once had a model of Dumbarton's *The Shield* as a centrepiece (though much easier at around 6a rather than 7b+, which would hurt the pride of those going to Dumby for the first time). Then in 2014, after the Commonwealth Games, a legacy fund allowed the building of the ultimate artificial bouldering venue at Cuningar, which is now a popular concrete/resin park for bloc-heads.

## DUMBARTON

In the 1960s Dumbarton's industrial bouldering took off in tandem with its first route developers Neil McNiven and Brian Shields. Along with Michael 'Silver' Connolly, they pioneered the boldest highball boulder problems in the 1960s, as well as hard technical lines up to British 6a, all in clumpy Vibram-soled boots, which is always worth recalling when you slip on a new pair of modern technical shoes. Classic highballs such as *B.N.I.* (5), *Route Royale* (5+), *The Switch* (5), and *Valhalla* (4) were climbed along with shorter technical problems such as *Nemesis* (5), *Hard Cheddar* (5+), and *PTO* (4+). In the 1970s new technical boots and an American-styled dynamic approach allowed some harder problems to fall such as *Gorilla* in 1978, Pete Whillance using a stack of shoogly cheat-stones to start (freed later by a jumping Pete Greenwell). Local legend Tam McAuley climbed *Tam's Route* (a desperate and bold 5+) and Willie Todd cranked out *Good Nicks* (6a). The 80s saw new levels with a headbanded *Gary Latter* nabbing the classic *Pongo* (7a) and Dave Cuthbertson, in 80s uniform 'vest and wee shorts' crushed out *Mugsy* (7a). John Christie turned up and slam-dunked the outrageous *High Flyer* (6c). In the 1990s Dumby pioneer Andy Gallagher slalomed up the slippery *Slap Happy* (7a) and started a fad for complicated traverses with the uber-classic *Consolidated* (7b+). Malcolm Smith pushed the power boundaries with *The Shield* (7b+) and *Pongo Sit Start*, the first 8a, which fell in1998. Meanwhile, a young 'Dumby' Dave MacLeod, honouring the 70s and 80s generation with a sporting ponytail, was eating up new classics such as *In Bloom* (7c+). Into the Millennium, he added Scotland's hardest problems of their time with the intricate *Sabotage* (8a) in 2003, the brutish *Pressure* (8b) in 2005, and the expansive geometry of *Sanction* (8b). Malcolm Smith was keeping tabs on this new school and quietly added his own power-fests of *Supersize Me* (8b) in 2005 and *Gutbuster (*8b+) in 2009. Since then, many linkups and new problems have been added by the campus-board generation, but the grade of 8c has up to early 2022 been elusive.

## CRAIGMORE

Craigmore had always been a popular climbing spot since the 1970s, ever since John Kerry bussed out to clean and garden the heavily vegetated walls. Underneath, he discovered a superb basaltic rock, which offered some good hard technical bouldering as well as bold solos. John produced a guide to the climbing and bouldering in the 'Glasgow Outcrops' guide by Highrange Sports (1975), printed by Rannoch Press out of Bearsden. The Carbeth hutters live nearby and the field above the crag used to be a campsite in the early 20th century, things found below the crag include old Tennent's cans, spades, and glass Camp Coffee bottles, so the crag has a long history of visitation. The old guide produced by John Kerry named some classic sectors such as 'Layback Crack' and 'Burnt Rock Amphitheatre' (Leech Wall area), listing a batch of routes up to British '6a' ('extremely severe'). In 1980s the route *Craig's Wall* was rope soloed by Craig Macadam (later freed by Dave MacLeod in 1997), upping the bar of technical vision which led to a focus on harder bouldering in the 90s by the likes of Andy Gallagher, Paul Savage, and Dave MacLeod. Good technical boulder problems began to be unearthed, such as *The Wizard*, *Andy's Arête*, *Terror Sit*, and all the *Jamie's Overhang* eliminates up to 7b, with Paul Savage casting a cruel eliminate eye to create the hardest problem here: *The Wizard Sit Direct* (7b+), which is rarely repeated.

## CRAIGMADDIE

Originally discovered as a climbing venue by Willie Gorman in the 1980s as a venue for micro-routes, Willie climbed the quarry crag and the high slabs as solos. These sandstone craglets on the south side of Craigmaddie Muir were inexplicably ignored as a bouldering venue until the early 2000s, when Pete Roy, Colin Lambton, John Watson and others began to open the territory to bouldering, with some fine lip traverses and cave problems. The rough sandstone needed some gardening and cleaning, but over time the venue has become very popular due to its relative accessibility and atmosphere akin to Northumberland. Ben Litster broke harder ground with *Alchemy* in 2008, and Mike Lee linked the long 7c of *Alakazaam* in 2012, then in 2021 David Elder climbed the big roof direct into *Alchemy* to give *The Magic* at 8a.

## CRAIGTON

Craigton is an old trad crag venue which was climbed on by John Mackenzie in the 1970s, with some of the shorter routes soloed as early highball bouldering problems, in particular the micro-route of *Machiavelli's Crack* at British 5c. It was then long ignored by climbers until Andy Gallagher and Darren Stevenson climbed the classic technical 7c arête of *'Far From the Maddening Crowd'* in the late 1990s. It was then ignored again until Fraser Harle unearthed the bouldering potential during the Covid lockdowns of 2020 and 2021. He opened the venue's potential with some dedicated brushing and landscaping, revealing a superb quality of rock and technical bouldering. With new problems cleaned and opened by Fraser, Brendan Croft, Kev Gibson, Peter Roy, Lewis Roy, Stuart Burns, and John Watson, this venue now has a circuit of superb problems on blond basalt. It is perhaps one of Glasgow's most expansive venues, and evidence of a continuing evolution of Glasgow's climbing scene: what was once perceived as a second-rate trad venue is now considered a prime bouldering circuit.

## ESOTERICA

In the 1980s Paul Laughlan used the Clochodrick Stone for training for the Tunnel Wall routes in Glencoe. The various link-up traverses of this wee Druid's bloc give a good workout up to around 7b. The Whangie was also used for similar sports stamina training along its traverse, which still offers extensions and harder possibilities. Esoteric venues around Lennoxtown were developed by John Watson (*The Dark Side*, 7a), Colin Lambton (*Stink Bug*, 7a, on the nearby Campsie blocs), and later Alex Gorham found the hidden roof-wonder of *Gordon Bombay* 7c in 2013. In 2020, Thom Davies added to *The Dark Side* with the logical direct 7c+ called *Solus Rex*. The old quarry at Court Knowe in Linn Park was always a micro-route venue before a few isolated boulder problems were added to the steeper ground on each side of the quarry, such as John Watson's *'There Is No Spoon'* (7a) from 1999. The usually-damp conglomerate walls of Cochno above Faifley were discovered in a dry spell after rhododendron bushes were chopped in 2014. Colin Lambton, Mark Dobson, and John Watson cleaned and climbed the majority of these problems in 2015, with the highlights being the pebble-pullers of *Mother India* (7a) and *Punjab Buffet* (7a). Small crags, boulders, and roofs continue to be found around Glasgow, often in the unlikeliest of places, such as Paisley's 'Andromeda Stane', developed by Joe Kelly in 2019. This unusual sandstone roof poking out in the middle of a small urban park gives the superb prow classic of *Andromeda's Horn* (6c+). The many quarries in the central belt area around Glasgow might provide more bouldering, and the higher crags in the hills have potential for a lot more. Going forward, the healthy imagination of younger generations will allow new linkups and creations to abound, so we don't expect any guidebook to have the final say.

★ *Kev Gibson on Pickpocket at Craigton*

## BLOC NOTES

This guide uses a combination of photo topos and textual descriptions to help you identify the boulder problems at each venue. The rest is up to you, but it is crucial before you climb that you check both your landings and your descent. Using a large mat helps give you confidence on highball problems, or those with uneven landings, but a good spot from a friend also helps. Remember, problems wander or traverse, so choose your matting carefully. Check round the whole boulder on arrival to identify your descent, or if it has a walk-off. Descents are mentioned in the text and topos if not self-evident. Travel and access descriptions are given in depth, but the notes at the start of each section may need explained. Below is an example, giving the nearest town and a postcode, which will get you to the general area (though it doesn't always send you exactly to the best parking). The parking is then listed as both a grid reference and a *What3Words* reference for your mobile phone apps. This mapping app gives each 3m-square on the planet a unique three-word code and is much easier than plugging in latitude and longitude coordinates! Whilst most map apps will allow you to plug in an OS Grid Reference, the *What3Words* app will need to be downloaded if you don't already have it. It also allows links to other map apps on Google and Apple, so can lead you right to the parking in their Sat Nav mode. The OS Grid references and *What3Words* are also given for the main blocs or central part of the venues (note, the three words can be scanned by your phone within the app's menu).

Access example for mobile apps:

| | | |
|---|---|---|
| Town | >>> | Strathblane |
| Sat Nav | >>> | G63 9LB |
| Parking | >>> | NS 52788 82501 /// negotiators.earlobe.gadgets |
| Blocs | >>> | NS 54999 83402 /// shimmered.shatters.headlight |

★ *Ross Henighan on Gorilla Warfare*

## BLOC NOTES >>>

Dumbarton Rock, 'The Rock', or 'Dumby' to boulderers, is one of Scotland's most concentrated venues for technical bouldering. Under the overhanging north-west crag lies a cluster of huge boulders with hundreds of top-quality problems within convenient reach of Glasgow. Dedication and perseverance are key to adapting to Dumby's unique climbing style but there are as many easy problems as hard problems and plenty for all ages and abilities. The geology very much informs the style of climbing as the rock is a fine-grained, compact and hard rock typical of volcanic 'Central Belt' basalt. It shears into planes and crisp edges that unfortunately glass over quickly with traffic, making Dumby notorious for its tenuous friction and the need for perfect atmospheric conditions (a bit like Fontainebleau). Consequently, Dumby is at its best in cool conditions in a dry spell, as sustained wet weather makes it very green. That said, it can dry extremely quickly (20 minutes or so after heavy rain) and friction is often at its best after a rain shower and drying wind when locals talk of 'sticky damp'.

## TRAVEL >>>

| Town | >>> | Dumbarton |
| Sat Nav | >>> | G82 1AJ |
| Parking | >>> | NS 40125 74440 /// lower.goes.poet |
| Blocs | >>> | NS 39909 74578 /// joined.bronze.others |

Dumbarton is 15 miles west of Glasgow city centre and is best approached from the south and east via the M8 motorway to cross the Erskine Bridge onto the A82. Dumbarton Rock's humped profile is easily visible on the north bank of the Clyde estuary. If approaching from the north, you will also be on the A82, so just follow signs into Dumbarton and then brown tourist signs to the castle at the bottom of Victoria Street and its continuation Castle Street. Park beside the castle at one of the various parking spaces and take the old path along the base of the north side of the rock. The boulders and main faces appear suddenly beside the River Leven's estuary.  As of 2021 Dumbarton Football Club's ground occupies the land in front of the approach to the crag, so it's worth checking when home games are played (usually a Saturday at 3pm) when it can be impossible to park. They don't mind climbers walking across their car-park grounds as a shortcut to the crag.

Regular trains run from Glasgow Queen St. low-level to Helensburgh Central and Balloch via Partick and Dumbarton. It takes about 25 minutes. Get off at Dumbarton East. Turn right at the bottom of the station, walk along 200m to turn left down Victoria Street to the castle. The Forth and Clyde Canal bike path runs from Glasgow along the Clyde and through Kilpatrick and Bowling to Dumbarton. Just after Bowling and Milton, the cycleway passes under the dome of Dumbuck and into residential Dumbarton. About one hour from Glasgow.

*Castle Grounds*

*SPORT WALLS*

*NORTH WEST FACE*

Descent

Descent

*Good Nicks*

*B.N.I.*

*Sabotage*

*SUCKER'S*

Descent

Descent

*Magsy Face*

*HOME RULE*

*The Shield*

*Hard Cheddar*

*Home Rule*

*Route Royale*

*PONGO*

*WARM-UP*

*Pongo*

*Consolidated*

TIDAL

*Eagle Slabs*

Descent

*Blue Meanie*

*EAGLE BOULDER*

*Zig Zag*

*Eagle Face*

TIDAL

*Shadow Wall*

*Gorilla*

Descent

*SEA BOULDER*

TIDAL

N

Parking

0m    5m    10m

## THE BOULDERS >>>

Dumby is home to many eliminates, link-ups and traverses which can't all be described in this guide. For a fuller listing, refer to *The Climber's Complete Guide to Dumbarton Rock*. The problems listed in this guide are the classic lines and should keep you busy for a while.

### Eagle Boulder

The giant prow boulder is first seen on the approach, under the main face. The boulder is named after a now-vanished eagle painted on the slabs in the 1960s (superseded by a Lion Rampant). Descent for all problems is via the ledges facing the main face, polished by a long history of many boots and shoes. It has four distinct facets with varying steepness from slabs to leaning walls to a flying northern roof and the famous *Gorilla* prow.

### Home Rule

The large, cubist bloc above the warm-up wall, with a high north face. This used to host 'Home Rule' graffiti in the 1970s. The problems are described in an anti-clockwise direction from the back chasm slabs round to a caved *Mugsy* sector, the *Home Rule* wall and the *Route Royale* walls.

### Warm-up Wall

This is the lower boulder wall under Home Rule, with a flat grassy landing, with walk-off descents. This is officially the least scary spot at Dumby and the best place to warm up.

### Sucker's Boulder

This is the boulder jammed in between the higher boulders of Home Rule boulder and the tall B.N.I. boulder. It is characterized by a leaning seaward face and a hanging ramp above. It sports the classic hard problem of *The Shield*, but also has easier perched slabs at the back right.

### B.N.I. Boulder

This is the tall boulder with various hanging walls above a walk-through cave sector adjoining the lower *Pongo* boulder. Originally named due to its reputation as being 'Bloody Nigh Impossible', the sectors comprise the walk-through cave, the hanging slabs of *B.N.I.,* and the perched slabs above the Pongo descent.

### Pongo Boulder

This is the lower boulder with the overhanging crack on the north-east face called *Pongo*. The westerly faces are slabbier in nature, steepening towards the walk-through cave sector at the end of the *Consolidated* traverse.

### Sea Boulder

The partly tidal bloc on the shore has four facets with arête problems.

EAGLE SLABS

ZIG ZAG SECTOR

## EAGLE SLABS

❑ 1. **Descent Route**                                        1
The polished staircase bounding the left arête is the easiest descent.

❑ 2. **Girdle Traverse**                                      3+
Traverse the slabs left to right at mid-height to finish up right to the ridge.

❑ 3. **Rankin's Bajin**                                       3
The slab 1m right of *Descent Route*, on right-trending holds to a small overlap .

❑ 4. **Soixante Neuf**                                        3+
Trend up right to a sloping ledge, then take the headwall through a letterbox.

❑ 5. **Pas Mal**                                              3+
Just left of the wee rock plinth. Climb up the slab to join the top of the ramp.

❑ 6. **Number One Route**                                     2
Start 1m right of the plinth, gain the left-trending ramp to the top.

❑ 7. **Left Direct**                                          3+
Right of the plinth to the ramp ledge, then direct up the wall via flakes.

❑ 8. **Centre Direct ★**                                      4
The hardest line on the slabs takes the slab direct at its blankest top section.

❑ 9. **Right Direct**                                         3+
Leads easily to a harder direct finish to the left of the flake of *No. 2 Route*.

❑ 10. **Number 2 Route**                                      3
Start as for *Right Direct* but move right up the corners and the high flake.

❑ 11. **Number 2 Direct**                                     4+
From a jug on the lip of the overhang, mantle into the groove above.

## ZIG-ZAG SECTOR

❑ 1. **Kev's Problem**                                        7a+
Sit start at two poor undercuts, pull on and gain the inset hold with the left hand. Slap through slopers to the jugs of *Pullover*.

❑ 2. **Pullover**                                             5
From the big jug on the lip 4m right along the roof, pop up and left to a flatty and pull onto the slab. Harder for the short.

❑ 3. **The Beastie**                                          6a
Stand under the big sloper at the wee nick on *Kev's Problem*, jump for the flat hold above the sloper and rock right onto the slab.

❑ 4. **Old Faithful**                                         5
The line just left of *Zig Zag*, climbed direct from finger-jugs on the lip onto the slab via finger layaways in a vague crack, rock onto the slab.

❑ 5. **Bust My Chops**                                        7a
Sit start at the low slopey shelf. Gain twin crimps above and then slap the left hand up to a right-facing corner sloper and twist up onto the slab.  Crossing the right hand to the corner sloper and finishing up *Pullover* is also good.

❑ 6. **Zig Zag ★**                                            4
Classic stopper. Pull over the roof onto the hanging slab via a protruding chalky jug, then step right then nervously back left through overlaps. Finish direct or up the easier groove leftwards. Various sit starts can be done.

SHADOW WALL

★ Steve Richardson on the 70s classic Tam's Route

❐ 7. **Bampot Arête** ★                                    6b+

Sit start the black arête from a very low position, gain the sloping ledge, then a right crimp. Slap to the left lip of the arête, go left and mantle the slab.

❐ 8. **Treasure Trail**                                    7b+

An excellent traverse. Start up *Bampot Arête*, then traverse left and low into the slot and crimp of *Bust My Chops*, finish low left and up *Pullover*.

## SHADOW WALL

The shadowed north roof and wall over a difficult landing. It is advisory to clean the top of the problems before an ascent. Multiple mats are useful, if not essential!

❐ 1. **Tam's Route**                                       5+

Takes the groove and walls right of *Bampot Arête*. Stand on the plinth and crank up the leaning groove on flatties. At the top of this, a slab sidepull and a high lip hold allows a rock-over left onto the slab. Finish left to *Zig-Zag*. A sit is 7a.

❐ 2. **Shadow** ★                                          7a

A classic hard highball first climbed by Andy Gallagher in 1992, this takes the overhanging black groove right of *Tam's Route*. Start from good edges at the back of the groove, crank backwards and left to a sloping hold and use a polished high step to go right to a sharp crimp. Hard pinches above lead to better holds and a reach to the flat holds at the base of the top slab. From here, balance onto the slab to finish up the ridge of the boulder.

❐ 3. **High Flyer**                                        6c

From the right side of the rocky ledge in the cave, position yourself carefully and make a committing jump up right to the chalky flat hold and continue right up jugs to mantle the lip.

❐ 4. **Smokescreen**                                       7c

Start at slot holds left of the big flat jug on the lip. Pull on and get a right heel on. Power up left to a hold, then slap right to a tiny ripple on a smooth ramp. Use a left undercut to go right again for the *High Flyer* jug and finish up this. A very committing problem.

❐ 5. **Pressure** ★                                        8b

From a heel hook start on the wee pillar at the back of the cave, climb through the big flat layaway and undercut back to the lip. Gain the slot and the flat jug then finish as for *Smokescreen*. FA Dave MacLeod, 2005.

❐ 6. **Firestarter** ★                                     8a

Heel-hook the juggy ledge on the cave lip (right hand on flange) and get hands established on poor crimps. Gain a left press hold in the groove and go again for an edge under the niche, then lunge for the slab lip and mantle. FA Dave MacLeod, 2004.

❐ 7. **Firefight**                                         8b

Cave start as for *Pressure* to a bat-hang semi-rest on the flat jugs at the lip, then finish right via *Firestarter*. May be harder than *Pressure* as it finishes up an 8a, but was given the same grade. FA Malcolm Smith, 2010.

GORILLA PROW

★ Ben Litster on Silverback

## GORILLA PROW

The sharp nose of the Eagle Boulder. A number of variations climb through and around the original problem, all superb exemplars of Dumby bouldering.

◻ 1. **Gorilla** ★        6b+

Pull on at twin crimps on the face and crank up to the right-facing layaway. Match this and then ape up left to the jugs on the lip. Rock over onto the slab.

◻ 2. **Gorilla Hanging Start**        7a

A hanging start from a good cave hold and a front crimp to gain the stand-up.

◻ 3. **Gorilla Warfare**        7a+

Goirlla to the lip, then turn the corner and climb along the slopey hanging lip[ to an iron-cross move to the jutting nose then mantle onto the slab.

◻ 4. **Gorilla Sit Start ('Neil's Extension')** ★        7b+

Sit start at a slopey front-face crimp facing rightwards and a left-hand cave sidepull. Slap back and left with clever heels and toes to gain the original.

◻ 5. **Silverback** ★        7c

From the *Gorilla* crimps move left to match a poor sloper and gain the incut hold on the arête. Boost for the jug on the nose to finish up *Gorilla*.

◻ 6. **King Kong**        8a

The classic complete link-up of *Neil's Extension* into *Silverback* then *Gorilla Warfare*. Eliminates the big lip jug at the top of *Gorilla*. FA Dave MacLeod, 2002.

◻ 7. **Shin Sekai**        6c+

The wall just right of *Gorilla* from an incut level with the layaway. Pull on and yard up left to a hold under the lip and mantle.

◻ 8. **Nature**        8a+

Sit start under *Gorilla*, on a sharp crimp under the roof and a right hand on a low face/lip hold. Gain a pair of crimps on the face and heel hook up right through crimps to the sharp hold then finish up *Shin Sekai*. FA Hamish Potokar, 2019.

◻ 9. **Hoop**        7c

Where the prow meets the ground. Gain a finger-jug and rock over to a crimp on top of the 'ear' feature. Go up left to a hard lip rockover.

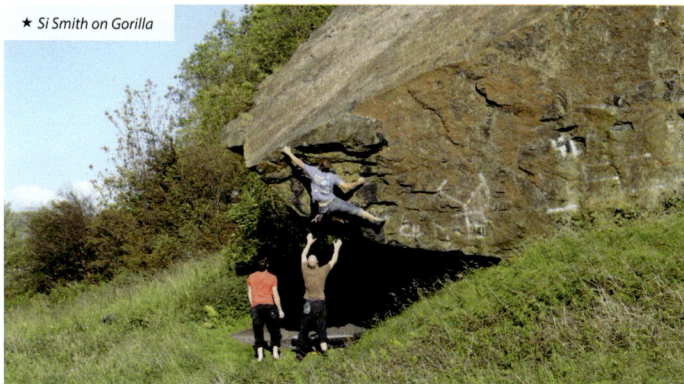

★ *Si Smith on Gorilla*

EAGLE FACE

BLUE MEANIE

## EAGLE FACE

The long face extending from the cave to a rock plinth by the tree-stump, before moving uphill by an orange face. Beware, the landing slopes badly and should be padded cleverly.

❐ 1. **Bingham's Wall**                                    7b+
Jump to the jug rail and go right to another jug. Gain a tiny right-hand crimp on the face and lunge to the lip. Rock onto the slab. FA Richard Bingham, 1999.

❐ 2. **Dressed For Success**                              7b+
Jump to jugs on the far left. Traverse the rail right to a crux drop-down at the *Supinator* crack, continue along micro-slopers to gain *2HB*.

❐ 3. **Supinator** ★                                      6a+
The central crack-line on the front face. A tricky start leads to better holds to a scary rock-over onto the slab. Aptly-named classic.

❐ 4. **2HB** ★                                            6a+
The angular groove left of the tree stump has a nippy move at half height to a triangular undercut, then up through some good crimps to jugs and a mantle.

❐ 5. **A Ford Flash**                                     7a
The orange groove above the tree. Gain a jug and cross to a crimp and reach up right to a press hold (common to *Torino Sun*). A high left-crimp and a hidden right undercut lead to jugs on top.

❐ 6. **Torino Sun** ★                                     6b
A modern classic. Step left off the plinth to a right-hand press to a left sidepull, go up right and then stretch left to juggy ledges.

❐ 7. **Oceans** ★                                         7c
The orange scoop from the crack holds, twisting left to an undercut. From here step left and cross through to a sloping crimp, gain holds above and commit to a protruding edge up and left.

❐ 8. **1990 Traverse**                                    7b
Sit start under the *Oceans* groove and layback up a vague crack. Traverse up and right on high crimps to a large flat hold. Continue rightwards to join *Blue Meanie*.

❐ 9. **Snappy**                                           6b+
Right of *Oceans*. Pounce to a sharp jug hold up and left of the *1990* crimp (committing). Layback the slot above and go right.

❐ 10. **Yappy**                                           6b+
Start 1m left of *Blue Meanie*, heading direct to a large undercling. Use this to yard up left to a distant jug, then a straightforward finish direct.

❐ 11. **Blue Meanie** ★                                   5
This committing classic takes the angular overhanging wall above the descent path slabs. Twist up to a large right-facing layaway niche and travel nervously left through hidden jugs to pull over the high lip.

❐ 12. **PTO**                                             4+
The black bulge right of *Blue Meanie*, with undercut reaches to reluctant jugs and pull over onto the descent ledges.

WARM-UP WALL

HOME RULE: VALHALLA

## WARM-UP WALL

This is the sea-facing vertical wall over a flat landing. Walk-off descents.

❐ 1. **Left Edge**     3
The left arête of the wall from the front, to a right-hand pinch and left-hand jugs.

❐ 2. **Friday's Fill**     3
The crack on the left wall.

❐ 3. **Friar's Mantle**     4+
The stepped groove and sloping ledges in the middle of the wall. A puzzling move at half-height provides the crux.

❐ 4. **Ungava**     4+
The wall right of *Friar's Mantle* from the jug ledge. FA Neil Macniven, 1960s. A dyno version missing the sidepull and pocket is 6a.

❐ 5. **Right Edge**     3+
A tricky start at the right-hand overlap to layback the edge on the right.

❐ 6. **Warm-Up Traverse**     4
*Left Edge* to *Right Edge* using the easiest line of jugs and crimps. A lower 6a version keeps under chin height, as low as possible.

## HOME RULE: VALHALLA

The bold, high walls of the Home Rule bloc are excellent tests of technique and nerve. The descent is 'The Beast' arête which feels easier going up than down! The slabs facing the crag are highball and sometimes need a good clean.

❐ 1. **The Switch**     5
Start as for *Valhalla* at the join of the boulders. Step down and left onto the hanging slab and climb the groove between *Valhalla* and *The Whip* (further left).

❐ 2. **Valhalla**     4
The committing shallow groove above the join of the two boulders. Bridge up over the chasm to a big sidepull jug, then finish directly up the edge of the thin slabby groove via a high-step and small holds.

❐ 3. **The Beauty**     4
The slabby wall and overlaps left of *The Beast*, right of *Valhalla*. Climb the slab to the overlap then trend right technically to step into the grooves.

❐ 4. **The Beast**     3
The highball juggy black arête at the back is also the descent from this boulder, taken on the cleaner *Valhalla* side.

❐ 5. **The Brute**     4
Start just right of *The Beast* and pull off the ground into the wee hanging groove using tricky foot edges, finish up *The Beast*. A sit start from the left is 5+.

❐ 6. **Valkyrie**     4+
Just right of *The Brute* is a hanging orange slab on the left side of the bulge above the smaller prop rock. Bridge or layback up into this to gain the slab.

HOME RULE: MUGSY

★ *Stewart Brown on Mugsy Static*

The cave roof leading underneath the boulder has a ramped northern lip with classic power problems. The key reference stand-ups can be linked from sit starts from various different problems, and it can get very confusing!

☐ 1. **Pas Encore**      5

Above the larger of the two prop rocks is a groove right of the bulge. Step on the right side of the prop boulder and pull steeply over left on a foot-jug to gain slopers on the slab, finish straight up the slab.

☐ 2. **Crimp!**      6b+

The jutting nose on its left side. From a standing position on the right of the prop bloc, gain a slot hold under the roof, then flat holds above. Gain a crimp above and just left of the arête and top out directly.

☐ 3. **Head Butt**      7a

Start standing on the block and pull into the corner right of the nose, using the left arête of the groove.

☐ 4. **Malky** ★      7b

Hang the starting jug of *Mugsy* but then take the sloping lip crimp with the right hand and go direct to the sloping shelf (heel-toe lock). A more modern method is to swing hard left to a frustratingly distant slopey sidepull (just below and left of the sloping shelf), then gain the shelf. Get standing on the shelf direct without the *Mugsy* jug out right.

☐ 5. **Mugsy** ★      7a

The centre of the face from the rail jugs. Jump start to a high right sloper, sort feet and gain a left undercut and throw for a distant jug. Finish left onto the slabs or right into the *Mestizo* groove. FA Dave Cuthbertson, 1983. A hanging 'static' start is a little harder and requires clever footwork.

☐ 6. **Mugsy Traverse**      7b

Start sitting on a small boulder on the left side of the cave. Pull on footless and traverse the line of sloping jugs right into the hanging start jugs, using a heel-toe lock to move into the original problem.

☐ 7. **Spam** ★      7c

A very low but classic sit start to *Mugsy*. Sit deep under the L-shaped sharp flake and twist to the poor twin crimps of *Mugsy Sit Start*, then slap for the jugs and finish up *Mugsy*. No block for feet.

☐ 8. **Mestizo**      6a

The arête. Swing up left to a good flattie, then use an undercut or slopey pinch to gain a good hold on the arête. Step into the groove to tiptoe up to an airy finish. FA Gary Latter, 1980.

☐ 9. **Mestizo Sit Start** ★      7a+

The overhanging sit start of the sharp arête. Sit start under the arête. From a slopey right-hand layaway and a left-hand cave crimp slap up left to the ledge, then gain the arête to finish up the original problem.

☐ 10. **Nice and Sleazy**      7c+

Quality modern link up starting up *Mestizo Sit Start* left along the shelf to the jugs then continue left to finish up *Malky*.

HOME RULE

ROUTE ROYALE & SUCKER'S

## HOME RULE FACE & ROUTE ROYALE FACE

The front faces of the boulder looking out to the River Leven. All are highball and require caution at the top for mantles. Descend via *The Beast* at the back.

❑ 1. **Physical Graffiti** ★ 6b

A highball classic! Start left of the centre and make a difficult move to gain a good high edge. High-step to further edges and step rightwards to good crimp below the lip, then mantle out with care. FA Gary Latter, 1980.

❑ 2. **Home Rule** ★ 6a

The central wall from the rail, through a blunt pinch or big rock-over to the higher handrail, traverse right to finish up via the arête.

❑ 3. **Home Rule High Traverse** 6b

Start as for *Home Rule*, but traverse left to join the *Mestizo* arête jug via small edges from the high handrail, then turn the corner and rock into the groove.

❑ 4. **Home Rule Low Traverse** ★ 7a+

Super-technical classic. From the arête of *Presence*, traverse low left to join *Mestizo*. A higher version is much easier at 6b.

❑ 5. **Presence** 5+

The unnerving right arête leans out over the drop before the handrail ... careful!

❑ 6. **Route Royale** 5+

The original came in from the Home Rule ledge to the left, swinging rightwards into the fault. Most now climb up the groove to a high sloping shelf on the left.

❑ 7. **Royal Arête** 6b

The highball arête taken direct, trending right at the top. Careful!

❑ 8. **The Whip** 5+

The highball slabby grooves right of *Royal Arête*. Pull on to jugs then tiptoe directly up to a nervy escape-step left near the top to good holds.

## SUCKER'S BOULDER: SHIELD FACE

The squeezed-in, leaning wall between Home Rule and B.N.I. boulders. The showpiece is the ultra-classic *Shield* problem.

❑ 1. **Toto** ★ 6a+

The slanting crack in the scoop on the left is a technical delight. Get established in the crack via polished footholds. Move up the crack to a high right-hand press crimp, allowing a nervy cross-step left to a jug. Finish trending left.

❑ 2. **Toto Sit Start** 7a

Sit start low right as far right as possible at small crimps under *The Shield*, in a cross-handed position. Traverse up and left to join the crack of *Toto*.

❑ 3. **Totality** 7b+

Climb *Toto Sit Start* and get established in the crack, reach right across the wall to a poor crimp, drop down to a sloping left-hand hold, then a crux sequence right leads to a mantle.

❑ 4. **The Shield** ★ 7b+

A famous Dumby power problem. Clamp the shield feature anywhere you can. Pull on with poor footholds, then lunge for the sloping lip and mantle. FA

SUCKER'S: SHIELD FACE

B.N.I. CAVE

Malcolm Smith, 1994.

❐ 5. **Power Pockets Sit Start**                7c
Using two low sloping crimps, gain *Power Pockets* and finish up this (the stand start is 6c). FA Dave Macleod, 2000.

❐ 6. **The Railings**                6b+
The popular hand-traverse of the slopey ledge. From the large pockets on the arête, pounce high left to a sloper edge on the lip, match, then traverse hard left, to finish with a mantle above *The Shield*.

## SUCKER'S BOULDER: SLABS

On the right of the boulder, perched under the B.N.I boulder, is a shaded slab, which when clean gives some good problems. Access by walking through the cave and round the back of the B.N.I. boulder.

❐ 7. **Mosca**                3+
The left arête of the slab in the gap, gained by squeezing along from the back corridor behind the B.N.I. boulder.

❐ 8. **Sucker's Slab**                4+
The thin slab left of the *Volpone* crack, straight up the centre on friction holds.

❐ 9. **Volpone Crack**                3
The intermittent crack on the right, on polished holds and foot smears.

## B.N.I. BOULDER

The tall boulder under the sports crag sector, it has a 'walk-through cave' sector, leading to a western overhang with perched tall slabs above it. Up the descent hole is another slabby wall facing the river.

❐ 1. **Chahala**                5+
Jump start the three 'campus' edges on the hanging north wall above the walkthrough cave. Finish by stepping right round onto the Pongo boulder.

❐ 2. **Chahala Sit Start**                8b
Sit start the arête by the prop boulder in the cave tunnel and clamp up this to join the original problem. No use of the prop boulder. Desperate backwards throwing and hard clamping. FA Dave MacLeod, 2007.

❐ 3. **Gutbuster**                8b+
One of Scotland's very hardest problems. Start at *Chahala SS* and follow this right to the kneebar rest on a spike at the base of the tiny hanging slab. Gain as much recovery here as possible before finishing up *Sanction* onto the slabs. Finish up *Imposter Arête* to celebrate. FA Malcolm Smith, 2008.

❐ 4. **Sabotage** ★                8a
Sit start at the western entrance to the cave walkthrough, right of the wee hanging slab, at two pinches. Undercut or kneebar backwards to gain a poor right-hand sloper, with a foot jam in the crack. Use arête holds to make a tricky horizontal heel-rockover sequence onto the slab. FA Dave MacLeod, 2003.

B.N.I. SABOTAGE

Pendulum

Good Nicks

B.N.I. SLABS

Sanction

☐ 5. **Sanction** ★                                             8b

The flying roof at the south entrance to the walkthrough B.N.I. cave. SS opposite the wee tunnel bloc, at holds on the left of a small hanging slab, and crank up into the flat holds above making use of a right heel on a small spike. From a high left spike, make a crux lunge to the inset hold below the lip and finish onto the slab via *Very Ape*. FA Dave MacLeod, 2007.

☐ 6. **B.N.I. Direct**                                          7b+

Stand on the stone plinth and start by hanging two crimps on the lip of the slab. Pull on and make a long morpho reach to a sharp crimp, get established on the slab and finish as for *B.N.I. Slab Direct*. A heel-hook on the lip out left might make this easier for some. FA Malcolm Smith, 1994.

☐ 7. **Good Nicks** ★                                          6b

A classic old peg crack up the groove right of the hanging B.N.I. slab. Climb the crack right to ledge jugs, then reach left for a distant crimp on the edge of the slab. Cross through onto the slab and finish up *Pendulum*.

☐ 8. **Pendulum**                                               4

The giant juggy flake above the ledges of *Good Nicks*. Climb the flake to pull left round the block onto the slab. Finish up the edge.

## B.N.I SLABS

There are two faces of hanging slabs: one on the left of the descent hole is a river-facing slab on the ledge above the descent hole of the Pongo boulder; the other on the right of the descent hole is the high undercut slab facing the Clyde estuary. The higher right slab has a long fall potential, so care is required.

☐ 1. **Astronomy**                                              3

Climb up through the descent hole to gain the balcony under the slab. This grooved rib on the left of the mezzanine slab is also the descent route. Step off a cracked pillar, climb to the top and descend the same.

☐ 2. **Deo Gratis**                                             4+

An excellent slab problem. Climb up through the descent hole to gain the balcony under the slab. Climb the central slab left of *Imposter Arête* to an undercut and a committing step up on a tiny foot edge to gain better holds above.

☐ 3. **Imposter Arête** ★                                      3+

Climb up through the descent hole to gain the balcony under the slab. The dramatic right edge arête of the slab above the descent route is straightforward but nerve-racking, climbed on small holds mainly on its left side.

☐ 4. **B.N.I.**                                                 5

Start at *Imposter Arête* and traverse diagonally across the orange slab, past a good central foothold, to the detached block on *Pendulum* and finish up this. A classic 60s highball thriller.

☐ 5. **B.N.I. Slab Direct**                                    5+

The most central challenge on the hanging slab. Start as for *B.N.I.* but from the good foothold move up to finish direct and centrally.

PONGO FACE

PONGO SLABS

## PONGO FACE

The steep, leaning wall facing northeast over a gravel slope. Fingery, butch and technical. Home to some absolute classic lines.

❒ 1. **Skint Knuckles**                                4

The right-hand corner/groove in the cave tunnel. Start using sidepulls left of the arête and layback up to mantle out right onto the ledges using the edge of the B.N.I. boulder.

❒ 2. **In Bloom** ★                                    7c+

Start matched at the arête left of *Slap Happy* and traverse right along the handrail via a crux drop-down move. If you can keep your feet on, continue along the rail and lunge to *Pongo* and finish up this. FA Dave MacLeod, 1998.

❒ 3. **Slap Happy** ★                                  7a

The classic slopey campus problem on the left side of the face. It boasts the most polished foothold at Dumby. From the jug flattie, gain a high sloping right-hand crimp and crank to a left-hand edge just under the lip, then another hold over the lip. Rock over using the corner of the B.N.I. boulder.

❒ 4. **Pongo** ★                                       7a

From the right side of the handrail, jump footless to the flange and then plant your feet. Continue up the powerful crack, with a crux slot move, to gain tenuous jugs at the top. Move left and rock up via holds on the nose feature, or continue leftwards to finish above *Slap Happy*. FA Gary Latter, 1980.

❒ 5. **Pongo Sit Start** ★                             8a

Sit start at the ledge, gain the niche and contort through to a right-hand crimp or pinch on the rattly bloc. A press move to the base of the flange (off polished footholds) leads to a hard crossover to better holds. Finish up the original *Pongo* crack. FA Malcolm Smith, 1998.

❒ 6. **Andy's Arête**                                  7a

Sit start the far-right arête and climb it with laybacks on the overhanging side. Use holds on the leaning wall as well. FA Andy Gallagher, 1990s.

❒ 7. **Supersize Me**                                  8b

Sit start right of *Andy's Arête* at the big pocket on the slab, climb left into *Pongo Sit Start,* then reverse the handrail of *In Bloom* and finish up *Slap Happy* (where it is easy to fail on the redpoint). FA Malcolm Smith, 2005.

## PONGO SLABS

❒ 1. **Sorcerer's Slab**                               3

Pull on at the point of the slab, by the shothole. Climb up near the left edge of the slab to ledges at the top. Descend right down the hole.

❒ 2. **Magic Wand**                                    3+

Start as for *Sorcerer's Slab* but go right a bit to a finger pocket, then aim straight up the centre via a blank section. FA Neil Macniven & Brian Shields, 1960s.

❒ 3. **Nemesis**                                       5

The nose at the base of the easy-angled groove is hard to surmount. From a poor right-hand finger lock crack, twist up to a good hold at the top of the nose and gain the easy groove leading to the top. FA Neil Macniven, 1963.

CONSOLIDATED

SEA BOULDER

## PONGO CONSOLIDATED

☐ 1. **Consolidated** ★                                     7b+

Stand start at sidepulls on the left nose. Slap up to the lip, then drop down low right to slopey holds. Traverse low right on slopers to the blunt arête under *Cheddar*. A crux sequence on white rock under the lip gains a big triangular hold, then slap up the arête of *Juggie* to finish. FA Andy Gallagher, 1994.

☐ 2. **EBGB**                                     6c

A higher traverse from the slabs around the nose to step onto to the low handholds of *Consolidated*, continue round to finish up *Hard Cheddar*.

☐ 3. **Narcosis**                                     5

Blind climbing up the faceted wall right of *Nemesis*, directly above the large, hidden undercut. Use sidepulls and blunt holds to step on. Gain a high right crimp to step up into the slim groove right of the bigger groove. Finish up this.

☐ 4. **Lunik**                                     4+

The scooped groove above the big flat slopers of *Consolidated*. Twist into the groove and climb the arête above right to the pointed apex. Technical.

☐ 5. **Cheddar**                                     4+

The undercut slab where the ground flattens out. From incut holds at the base of the hanging slab, pull on to climb directly to the apex via a delicate move.

☐ 6. **Hard Cheddar** ★                                     5+

A classic technical problem. Pull on as for *Cheddar* but immediately travel right along slopey flanges on the bottom lip of the slab to a hard move to gain a ledge above the arête of *Juggie*, then finish up the slab. FA Brian Shields, 1960s.

☐ 7. **Juggie**                                     4

The hanging arête just left of the descent route. Start at the big polished triangle hold and climb the arête onto the slab. A direct sit start is 6b+.

## THE SEA BOULDER

An easy scramble groove to a lookout ledge marks the northern side of this partly tidal boulder, which is also the descent.

☐ 1. **White Streak**                                     6b

The wall facing the stadium (no arêtes). Gain the crimps high on the wall via a triangular hold near the right arête. Lunge to the top left ledge (it's not a jug).

☐ 2. **Steptoe** ★                                     3+

The arête climbed mainly on its right side, without the use of the old lump of tubular lead. FA Neil Macniven, 1960s.

☐ 3. **Red Streak**                                     6a

The wall just right of *Steptoe*, no holds on *Chowbok* to the right nor the lump of lead! The crux is a technical step-up via a crimp to a higher crimp.

☐ 4. **Chowbok**                                     3+

The cracked seaward wall in the centre to a pod and mantle at the top. FA Michael Connolly & Brian Shields, 1960s.

☐ 5. **Erewhon**                                     4+

The super-polished right arête, using undercuts on the right wall and faith in feet! Jugs appear at half-height and the top is easier. FA Neil Macniven, 1960s.

★ *Silver's Route on the Sea Boulder*

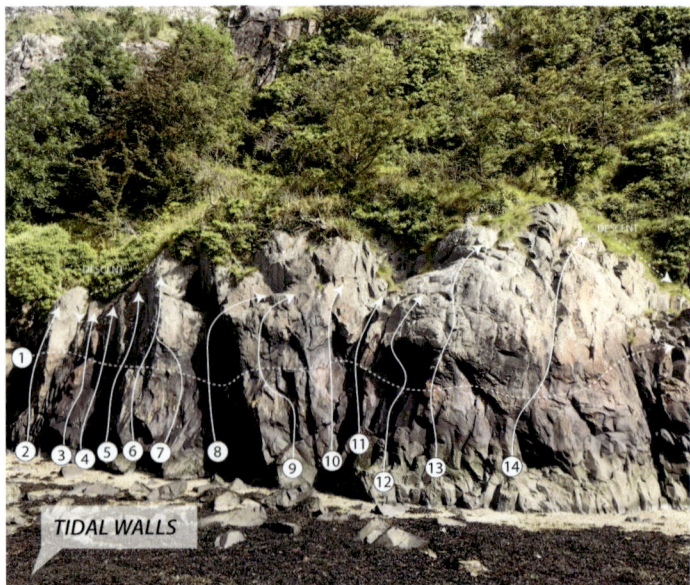

TIDAL WALLS

❐ 6. **Commercial Route**      4

The corner just right of *Erewhon*, stepping onto the arête and right wall.

❐ 7. **Wednesday Wall**      4+

The slab and arête, using holds on both, to gain flatties and sidepulls above.

❐ 8. **Silver's Route**      3+

Sidepulls and smears up the slabby wall. A desperate sit start is 6c+.

❐ 9. **Silver Rib**      3+

Pull onto the right arête/rib via smears and climb direct to top ledges.

❐ 10. **Gardner's Girdle**      4+

Traverse anti-clockwise low around the boulder. FA Davie Gardner, 1960s.

## TIDAL WALLS

Further right at the end of the crag, a scramble leads down to the shore. The central bay of the traverse has a good wall of various straight-up problems over gravel, when the tide is out. Beware fast-returning tides!

❐ 1. **The Sea Traverse**      5

Traverse the low sea walls from the metal ring to the east end, there and back again, staying as low as possible on the best rock.

❐ 2. **Left Edge**      4

Take the left arête to a blank top, turned on right at half height for feet.

❐ 3. **One-piece Puzzle**      5+

The slopey brown nose is taken direct from an incut. How to get off the ground?

❐ 4. **Slab & Corner**      3

Step onto the slab delicately and trend right to a crack finish up left to ledges.

❐ 5. **Corner Wall**      3

Step into the corner then up right onto ledges, then back left via crack holds.

❐ 6. **Ledge Wall**      3

Climb corner then right onto the wall to a foot-ledge and trend left using crack.

❐ 7. **Rib Climb**      4+

Climb the blunt rib to ledges and join *Ledge Wall* at half height.

❐ 8. **Black Slab Crack**      4

Slab and corner crack to swing right round arête at the top, traverse off right.

❐ 9. **Flexation**      5

From a sloping ledge step onto the arête foothold and top out direct.

❐ 10. **The Groove**      3

Step awkwardly onto a ramp and move more easily up right via jugs.

❐ 11. **Corner Crack**      2

Bridge up the corner using holds on both sides. Useful descent.

❐ 12. **Snaking Cracks**      3

The scooped cracks right of the corner. Descend *Corner Crack*.

❐ 13. **Red Rib**      4

Step up the brown/red blunt nose trending right, then back left to higher ledges.

❐ 14. **Right-hand Groove**      2+

A steadier problem taking the right-hand groove to good jugs. Descend right.

# ◻ COCHNO STONES

★ Colin Lambton on Cochno Prow

## BLOC NOTES >>>

A few nice blocs requiring a long dry spell, but with some terrific grit-like problems on pebbles, rough slopers and crimps. It is an esoteric venue, so do take note the crags face north and are green after rain and may need cleaning to get the best out of them. They are best on a fine, breezy summer day.

## TRAVEL >>>

| | | |
|---|---|---|
| Town | >>> | Faifley |
| Sat Nav | >>> | G81 5QW |
| Parking | >>> | NS 50343 73989 /// awaiting.ruffling.diagram |
| Blocs | >>> | NS 50405 73975 /// mend.steers.chart |

Bus to Faifley and walk up paths. By car: take the A82 west out of Glasgow through Drumchapel to the Kilbowie roundabout at Duntocher, just west of the Braidfield Hotel. Take the north Hardgate exit and follow the road uphill to Hardgate roundabout. Take the first exit west and then immediately right (at the pub) up Cochno Road (if you go past the petrol station you've gone too far). Go steeply uphill for 1km to open country and a fork in the road, bearing right past Cochno farm and houses for 600m to a sudden right turn, then turn left into ample parking. The blocs are under a small bluff at the south end of the parking, obscured by forestry in summer, but more easily seen in winter. The closest bloc is the wee wall of ❏ **West Wall** visible from the parking. 25m east of this is the 4m roof of ❏ **Cochno Prow**. Just east of this is the longer ❏ **Smithless Wall**. Beneath this is a twin set of slabs, the east one being the orange slab of the ❏ **Heart Stone**. The most easterly, undercut, caved wall (and the tallest) is the ❏ **Cochno Wall**.

## THE PROBLEMS >>>

❏ 1. **West Wall**                                                     6a
The short west wall from a sit start via small pockets and crimps.

❏ 2. **West Wall Arête**                                          3
The short arête laybacked to jugs at the top. A sitter on the blunt base is 5.

❏ 3. **Fallen Tree Crack**                                     6b
FA Brendan Croft, 2019. Between Cochno Prow and West Wall is a short buttress with a fallen tree propped against it. Behind the tree is a thin finger crack . Climb this to a large sloper on the right and top out.

❏ 4. **Cochno Pocket**                                          5
Sit start Cochno Prow and climb the right wall of the short prow feature, using ledges and a lateral pocket.

❏ 5. **Cochno Prow** ★                                          6b
Sit start the cave of the prow direct to pockets and gain slopers on the right wall before trending left via a crux move through a high arête sloper and a pebble on the left wall to gain the top.

❏ 6. **Smithless Arête**                                        5+
Sit start the short right arête of Smithless Wall via knobby features on the arête and for feet.

# COCHNO STONES

18
17
16

12
11
10
-13-
9
15    8
14    7
      6

        5
        4.

East

North    South

West

3.

2.    -1

**P**

Faifley

Auchnacraig
House

Hardgate

18

17   16

COCHNO WALL

❑ 7. **Colin's Problems** 6a+

Sit start *Smithless Arête* but climb left to a technical reach to crimps on the wall then to jugs at the top. No higher arête allowed.

   ❑ 7a. A stand start to the wall from crimps. 5
   ❑ 7b. A dyno from the crimps to the top. 4+
   ❑ 7c. An eliminate leftwards finish from the top layaway is 6b+

❑ 8. **Smithless Wall 1** 5+

The central wall via a righthand sidepull right of the red streak and a left sidepull left of red streak. A technical sequence leads to a pop to the lower right ledge and mantle.

❑ 9. **Mexican Necktie** 6b

The wall just right of the red streak. Crouch start at a good sidepull and take a technical sequence up left to a high sidepull/gaston, then snap to the ledge on the right.

❑ 10. **Red Streak Direct** 6b+

Start crouched directly under the red streak using pockets. Climb directly up the red streak to the high ledge (without using the lip on the right) and mantle.

❑ 11. **Smithless Wall 2** 6a

The left side of the long wall via a left sidepull and high crack to ledges.

❑ 12. **Left Wall** 2+

The left side of Smithless Wall taking the easiest line on jugs on the far left of the wall, then trending right at top to mantle the right ledge.

❑ 13. **Covert-19** 6c+

Eliminate traverse from *Smithless Arête* on low undercuts left to a sidepull, gain an undercling and a toe hook to drop into the high right sidepull. Get the deep pocket under *Red Streak* and finish direct. FA Colin Lambton, 2019. Further eliminate traverses can be contrived.

❑ 14. **Orange Arête** 6a

Heart Stone. Sit start the short arête and climb up the steep right side via a jug to a mantle.

❑ 15. **Warren Buffet** 5+

Climb the face of the orange 'Heart Stone' using a large pebble on the left. Without the pebble, it's 6b+.

❑ 16. **Mother India** 7a

Cochno Wall. Sit start *Punjab Buffet* but gain a right-hand pocket, then a technical use of two pebbles above leads to a crux snatch to a small ledge under the top, mantle to finish. FA John Watson, 2015.

❑ 17. **The Punjab Buffet ★** 7a

Cochno Wall. Sit start on the right at a left-hand gaston and right crimp. Travel left with tricky feet and hands into the high gaston sloper, then gain a poor right pebble and slap to the top. FA John Watson & Colin Lambton, 2014.

❑ 18. **Shezan** 5

Cochno Wall. The left wall, jumping to the big slopey sidepull from the far left, match and reach up right to the top.

★ Fraser Harle on Liberator Crack

# CRAIGTON

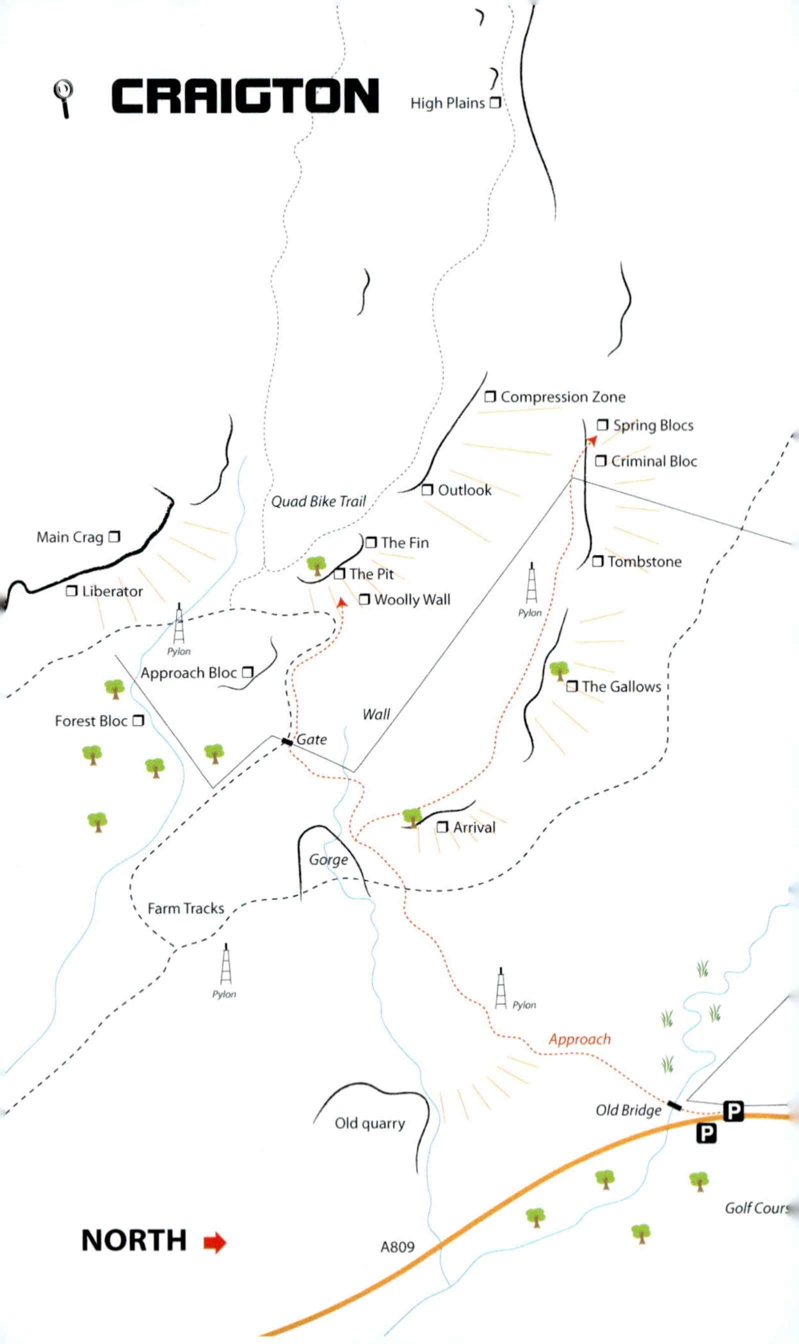

High Plains □

Compression Zone □

Spring Blocs □

Criminal Bloc □

□ Outlook

*Quad Bike Trail*

Main Crag □

□ The Fin

□ The Pit

□ Liberator

□ Woolly Wall

□ Tombstone

*Pylon*

□ The Gallows

*Pylon*

Approach Bloc □

*Wall*

Forest Bloc □

→ *Gate*

□ Arrival

*Gorge*

Farm Tracks

*Pylon*

*Pylon*

*Approach*

Old Bridge

Old quarry

P

P

NORTH →

A809

*Golf Course*

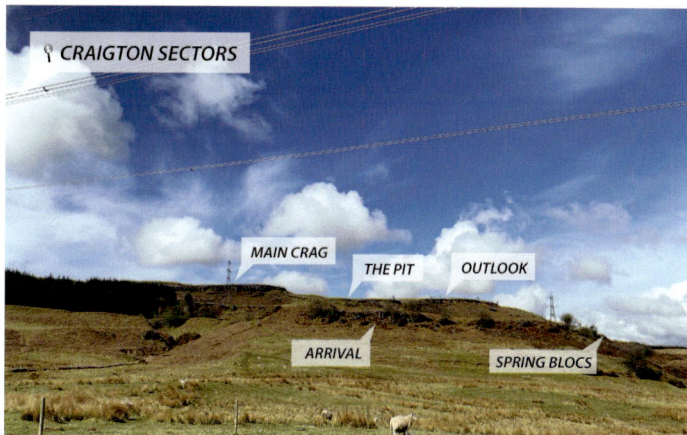

CRAIGTON SECTORS

MAIN CRAG

THE PIT

OUTLOOK

ARRIVAL

SPRING BLOCS

## BLOC NOTES >>>

Craigton is becoming one of Glasgow's best bouldering venues, with a fine northerly outlook over the Southern Highlands. There are loads of blocs, arêtes and walls on scattered escarpments. It was first climbed on in the 1970s and the late 1990s. The newer bouldering was mostly cleaned by Fraser Harle, Brendan Croft and John Watson in 2020/21, revealing quality blond basalt rock. It is best in spring and autumn out of bug & bracken season.

## TRAVEL >>>

| Town | >>> | High Craigton |
|------|-----|---------------|
| Sat Nav | >>> | G62 7HB |
| Parking | >>> | NS 52490 77307 /// receive.sing.plodding |
| Blocs | >>> | NS 51702 76912 /// doctor.regress.trespass (Pit Sector) |

Take the A809 north out of Bearsden on Stockiemuir Road, through the roundabout at the BP garage into open country. 500m after High Craigton, park in small laybys on the left or right below the main car park for Hilton Park Golf Course, but don't block any gates. Enter through the west double gate, turn left to skirt the forestry fence to cross the old bridge. Hop the gate/wall and strike directly uphill to the first pylon. From here, cross a field and take a rising path on the right of a small gorge and left of a small escarpment of the ❏ **Arrival** sector. From the plateau, you can strike right to the ❏ **Spring/Criminal** sector beyond the pylon over the end of the old wall. For ❏ **The Pit** sector, cross the wee burn to the main farm track and go through the gate and up to the bend in the track. This is a good base point for exploring the area. Following the track left leads to the ❏ **Main Crag** sector. Right of *The Pit* sector, the escarpment continues to ❏ **The Outlook** sector and ❏ **Compression Zone**. Further north on the plateau is the highball ❏ **High Plains** sector. The approach is a twenty-minute hike to the first sectors, with further limits of the plateau taking somewhat longer.

ARRIVAL

Hidden Bloc

Heptapod

Fridge Bloc

Moai Bloc

Gallows 50m

★ Fraser Harle on Bring Up the Bodies

THE GALLOWS

① ② ③ ④

## ARRIVAL >>>

The first small escarpment above the first pylon has a few hidden blocs below a line of very old and gnarled rowan trees. The walls are more evident in winter.

❏ 1. **Toka Huna** 6b+

Low start the blunt left arête on the far left bloc under ancient rowan trees.

❏ 2. **Squeezed** 6a

Stand start the right arête on the same bloc, above the horizontal tree.

❏ 3. **Zanussi** 4

The wee pillar bloc seen on approach. Climb the front left face from a crouch.

❏ 4. **Smeg** 6b

Sit start the right face via bearhugs and smears. FA Kev Gibson, 2021.

❏ 5. **Heptapod** 6a

The central lip bulge 15m right of *Smeg*. Sit start left, move right to mantle onto the slab and jugs, using a cup hold near the right corner. FA John Watson, 2021.

❏ 6. **Abbott** 5

Sit start the low crack on the right of the lip at a horizontal break and snatch up right to good holds and gain jugs, drop off. FA John Watson, 2021.

❏ 7. **Moai** 5+

The leaning pillar in a chasm/cave 20m right again. Crouch start up its right arête to reach for the left side, mantle onto the ledges. FA John Watson, 2021.

## GALLOWS BLOC SECTOR >>>

The complex set of walls in the scree amidst all the ferns about 100m right of the Arrival sector. The main bloc is the pillar underneath a tree stump.

❏ 1. **Gallows Arête Left** 4

Sit start the left arête and climb it, it's nice and balancy.

❏ 2. **The Gallows** 5+

Sit start left of the ramp to a good horn jug, trend right to a big pocket and then rock back left onto the horn to a thin and balancy finish to jugs.

❏ 3. **Bring Up the Bodies** ★ 6c

Sit start at the ramp and gain a good right-hand edge and a left-hand slot up the ramp. Pounce to a right crimp just under the lip and rock up directly through the big pocket to better holds. No horn for feet and no right arête. Summit left of the tree stump. FA Fraser Harle, 2021.

❏ 4. **Gallows Arête Right** 3+

Climb the right arête from a stand start, finish directly.

## APPROACH BLOC >>>

The bloc on the hill above the track after the gate. FAs Brendan Croft, 2022.

❏ 1. **Uitwaaien** 5+

Sit start on the left side of the boulder.

❏ 2. **Flurry** 4

The right face, finishing up the juggy crack.

❏ 3. **Squall** 5

The right arête on the right face of the boulder.

## MAIN CRAG

Wave Wall

Shield

Tess

Hand of God

Far From ...

Doddle

Olmec

Liberator

Font Blocs

Approach

★ Fraser Harle escaping the ferns on Tess

## LIBERATOR SECTOR

1
2
3
4
5
6

## FOREST BLOC >>>

A steep bloc in the woods south of the stream 50m left of the Approach Bloc.

⧠ 1. **Tambowie**     6b+

Sit start the left side of the wall. FA Fraser Harle, 2022.

## MAIN CRAG >>>

The highest escarpment featuring a number of old traditional routes, centred round the cracked buttress of *The Screaming* (E2). The left end is marked by a messy old quarry, the right end by a square pinnacle (*The Shield*), with associated blocs, walls, and arêtes all along the crag. Some of the problems are highball and require a bold, confident approach, and clean your topouts!

## HAND OF GOD BLOC >>>

The furthest left pinnacle bloc.

⧠ 1. **Hand of God**     6a+

Sit start the bloc on the very left of the outcrop, use anything to the top. 6b without the left arête. 6c with no arêtes. FAs by Brendan Croft, 2021.

## OLMEC BLOC >>>

A pinnacle 20m right of the quarry. FAs by Brendan Croft, 2021.

⧠ 1. **Inuksuk**     6a+

The centre of the wall to an undercut hold, then a long reach to the ledge.

⧠ 2. **Inuksuk Arête**     5+

The left arête.

⧠ 3. **Olmec**     5+

The highball front face. Once at the big hold trend right to finish as for *Inuksuk*.

⧠ 4. **Olmec Direct**     6b+

Direct finish to *Olmec* with a sloping top out. Brush the top before an ascent.

## LIBERATOR SECTOR >>>

Just left of the main crag there is a small amphitheatre with a clean arête pinnacle on the left, a central cracked wall, and a right-hand wall.

⧠ 1. **Machiavelli's Crack**     5+

The crack system under the tree, sticking to the right crack to pass the tree. FA John Mackenzie, 1970s.

⧠ 2. **Tess**     6a

The arête on its left side also using the crack on the left. FA Brendan Croft, 2021.

⧠ 2a. **Tess Eliminate ★**     6b+

The arête without the crack. An excellent eliminate version. FA Lewis Roy, 2021.

⧠ 3. **Jude**     6b

The right-hand side of the *Tess* arête. Gain a big hold on the right and then slap up to mantle onto this. FA Brendan Croft, 2021.

⧠ 4. **Liberator Crack ★**     6a

The excellent curving crack on the slabby wall, also using holds on the right wall to a mantle at the top onto ledges. FA Brendan Croft, 2019.

🔭 *MAIN CRAG*

The Screaming

1

2

🔭 *DODDLE SECTOR*

1  2  3  4  5  6

🔭 *SHIELD BLOC*

1  2  3  4

❏ 4a. **Liberator Crack Direct**                                      6a+

An equally good but harder version taking the crack direct with no right wall holds, mantle direct at the top. FA Fraser Harle 2021.

❏ 5. **Revelator**                                                          6b+

Low start at the flake just right of *Liberator Crack*. Delicately traverse right through the slanting crack to gain a pocket, then make big moves to top out directly on slopers. *Liberator Crack* is out. FA Brendan Croft, 2021.

❏ 6. **Mantleshelf Wall**                                             5+

The pinnacle wall and slab just down and right of *Liberator Crack*. Use good holds to mantle left onto a wee ledge, then climb onto the highball top slab.

## MAIN CRAG SECTOR >>>

❏ 1. **Far From the Maddening Crowd** ★               7c

The classic and highball arête, originally given E6 6c. Climb the blunt right arête of the pinnacle, just left of the main crag. FA Andy Gallagher, 1990s.

❏ 2. **Wavy Wall**                                                        6a+

Good highball arête and wall 20m right of *The Screaming* route. Named after the wavy feature on the rock. Can be climbed as a jump-off problem as well.

## DODDLE SECTOR >>>

A nice short wall onto a ramp under a headwall. FAs by Brendan Croft, 2021.

❏ 1. **Cakewalk**                                                         6a

A good problem. Sit start the left arête at a large sidepull and a right crimp. Gain the lip and traverse left to gain a large hold.

❏ 2. **Breeze**                                                            6a

Sit start the blunt arête just left of *Layback Crack*. Gain a deep incut crimp and slap left to mantle and traverse off right.

❏ 3. **Layback Crack**                                                5

Sit start, and layback up the flake onto the ramp and traverse off right.

❏ 4. **Flared Crack**                                                   5+

Sit start the flared crack up to good holds and traverse right.

❏ 5. **Scooped Arête**                                                6a+

Sit start the arête on the right.

❏ 6. **Doddle Traverse**                                            6a

Good lip traverse, up *Cakewalk* to lip, traverse right to finish up *Scooped Arête*.

## SHIELD BLOC SECTOR >>>

The pinnacle at the right end of the main crag. FAs by Brendan Croft, 2021.

❏ 1. **Trident Left Edge**                                           5

The left edge of the pinnacle.

❏ 2. **Trident Direct** ★                                            6c

Good crimpy, technical climbing. Start at the centre of the bloc at its lowest point and follow the thin crack to a central top out. The shield feature is out.

❏ 2a. **Trident Left Fork**                                          6b+

Same as *Trident Direct,* but escape left at the top using the slanting crack.

FONT BLOC

1 2 3 4 5

THE PIT BLOC

1 2 3 4 5 6

★ *Fred Carrick on Lightning Tree Crack © Fraser Harle*

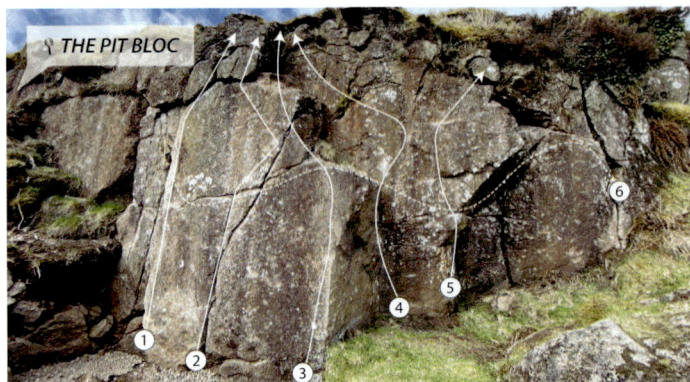

❏ 3. **Shield Right Edge** 5

This problem takes the right arête past the shield feature.

❏ 4. **Sion's Climb** 6b

About 10m right of the Shield Bloc. Climb the wall using a thin crack to the horizontal break, then navigate the crux slopey top out.

## FONT BLOC SECTOR >>>

The small, isolated blocs at the base of the slope under the main crag. The main bloc is the rounded, slabby 'Font' Bloc, with smaller blocs to the back and left of the Font bloc. FAs Brendan Croft, 2021.

❏ 1. **Italics** 4

Sit start at the eye-shaped hold and climb up.

❏ 2. **Calibri** 6a

Stand start at the rounded layaway with a right hand on a crimp and rock over.

❏ 3. **Helvetica** 5

Stand start and pad up using two crimps over the lip.

❏ 4. **Arial** 6b+

Stand start on the good foothold in the groove, a left hand on a crimp, a right on slopers. Gain a scooped hold and slap for the top.

❏ 5. **Verdana** 6a

Sit start on the very right of the boulder, slap left to the shield-shaped jug and continue left to rock over at the scooped hold on *Arial*.

❏ 6. **Garamond** 5

Sit start on the right, gain the shield and top out directly above.

❏ 7. **Which Sheep?** 6a

On the Sheep Bloc, a small boulder left and back from the Font Bloc. This takes a left to right traverse along the lip, finishing around the corner.

❏ 8. **Far from the Maddie Crowd** 6a

Sheep Bloc. Sit start right and traverse the lip to rock over at a good hold.

❏ 9. **The Lamb** 6b

The tiny overhang boulder, just left of the Sheep Bloc, gives a fun 6b sit start.

## THE PIT BLOC >>>

The bloc cluster and walls just above the switchback track below the Main Crag. A good place to meet friends and start out.

❏ 1. **Sprite Arête** 6a

Climb the sharp left arête using the crack on the right as well.

❏ 1a. **What Lies Beneath** 6c

An eliminate of *Sprite Arête*. Sit start the sharp left arête with no recourse to central holds. Layback and smear to a lunge at the top. FA Stuart Burns, 2021.

❏ 2. **Lightning Tree Crack ★** 6a

Smear and layback up the wall using the crack for hands, finishing direct. No left arête or feet out right. FA Lewis Roy, 2020.

❏ 3. **Right Arête** 4

Climb the short right arête and mantle onto the higher ledges.

WOOLLY WALL

THE FIN SECTOR

OUTLOOK LEFT

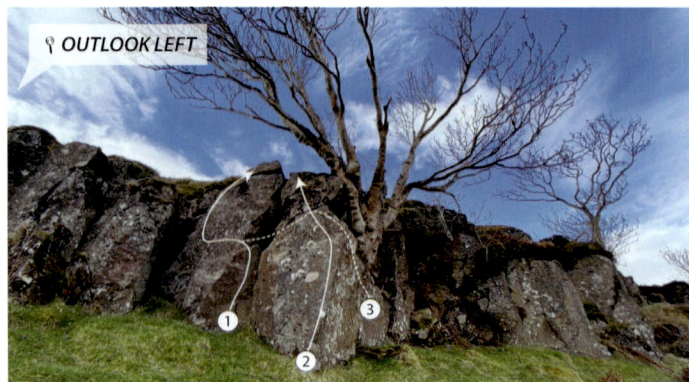

⬚ 4. **Right Corner**                                           4+
Bridge up the corner and use a right gaston to mantle onto ledges.
⬚ 5. **Blue Jet**                                               6c
Sit start finger ledges and gain double slopers on the central wall; use a sidepull
to gain a high left hold and trend right to a block with a white dot.
⬚ 6. **Spider Traverse**                                        6a+
From the far right, traverse left down through *Blue Jet* to finish up *Sprite Arête*.
FA Fraser Harle, 2020.
⬚ 7. **Mariana**                                                5+
Sit start on the left of the hidden pit just below *The Pit* wall and mantle the slab.
⬚ 8. **Warm-Up Wall/Bo-Pop**                                    4
30m right of The Pit under a small tree.

## WOOLLY WALL >>>
The low bloc just below *The Pit*, seen on approach.
⬚ 1. **Le Frêne Sauvage**                                       6c
Sit start the wee cave at the back of *Woolly Face*.  No feet out right.
⬚ 2. **Woolly Face Sit**                                        5
Sit start the left front face to the blunt edge and mantle.
⬚ 3. **Woolly Face Traverse**                                   6b
Right to left frontal low traverse on rails.
⬚ 4. **John's Slab**                                            6a
The cleaned perched slab to the right, a tricky mantle from good holds.

## FIN SECTOR >>>
The beak-shaped fin of rock right of *The Pit* sector on the escarpment.
⬚ 1. **The Fin Left**                                           P
Climb the arête left of the niche roof to the top wall.
⬚ 2. **Downfall**                                               5+
From within the niche behind the low fin, climb direct through the roof (bottle
required).
⬚ 3. **The Fin**                                                5+
Climb the fin's right edge with assistance from the crack on the right.
⬚ 4. **The Fin Right**                                          4
Climb the right wall by using big and small cracks.

## OUTLOOK >>>
The walls and blocs further right, under a four-pronged rowan tree. FAs by
Fraser Harle, 2020.
⬚ 1. **Micro Soft Arête**                                       5
The left arête started from the right side.
⬚ 2. **Right Arête**                                            5
The right arête.
⬚ 3. **Micro Soft Arête Extension**                             6a
From the tree, climb up left, then downclimb the crack to finish left.

COMPRESSION ZONE

1 2 3 4 5 6

HIGH PLAINS

1 2 3 4

★ Fraser Harle on Welcome to Lago © Fraser Harle

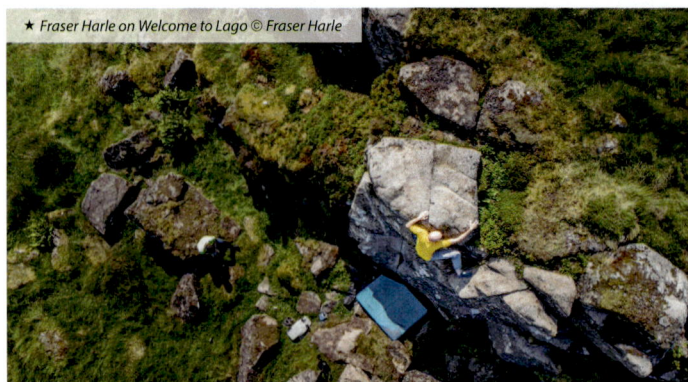

## COMPRESSION ZONE >>>
A bit further right is a trio of walls split by a tree.

▢ 1. **Peripheral Cracks**                                     3
This problem takes the wall left of the curving crack.
▢ 2. **Atmospherics**                                          4+
The slabby wall right of the crack through a horizontal crack.
▢ 3. **The Bell**                                              5
This problem takes the central wall's left arête to a mantle.
▢ 3a. **Hyperbarics**                                          5+
Same start but trend right through the capping stone.
▢ 4. **Three-Pocket Problem**                                  6a
The central wall's right arête, using three small pockets on the wall to gain a tricky mantle through the perched bloc on top.
▢ 5. **Arthralgia**                                            7a
A right to left sit start traverse across the right wall, using hard presses and slopers. FA Lewis Roy, 2020.
▢ 6. **The Bends**                                             5
Sitter from a low start on the farthest right edge, through arête right of the main face, trending left at the top.
▢ 7. **Displacement**                                          4
The right arête on the narrow side face of the right-most bloc.

## HIGH PLAINS SECTOR >>>
Further north on the plateau, about 10 minutes' walk uphill from Compression Zone and along a vague quad bike farm track, is a 5-metre grooved buttress. It is a little highball, so big mats and spotters may be worth it for the trip. From the Main Crag plateau it can be spied on the north side approach to the vague summit of the hill.

▢ 1. **Mordechai**                                             5+
The perched low wall up left traversed from left to right.
▢ 2. **Paint the Town Red ★**                                  6a
The highball left arête and wall gaining undercuts in the top perched block to a mantle.
▢ 3. **Welcome to Lago ★**                                     6a
The central crack trending right to a bulge then pulling back left into the hanging groove above half height.
▢ 4. **The Stranger**                                          5
From the small boss/shoulder on the right arête, step left into the capped groove and surmount the bulge.

★ John Watson on Crack Thief © Fraser Harle

SPRING BLOCS

CRIMINAL BLOC

## SPRING BLOCS >>>

Superb twin blocs with stunning rock. A bubbling spring can be heard beneath.

☐ 1. **Pansy**              5+

From a left slot and big right undercling, pull on left to the lip, then use shallow pockets to reach out left to a good hold and a mantle.

☐ 2. **Pansy Direct**          6b

From the big undercling, gain the holds over the lip, then reach up right to a good edge and mantle onto the slab direct.

☐ 3. **Snowdrop**          7c

Sit start the central roof at undercuts and gain the lip, then mantle over using tiny crimps. Trend left onto the slab. The decent, diagonal groove over the bulge is out. FA Lewis Roy, 2021.

☐ 4. **Speedwell** ★          6b+

Crouch start hard left under *Pansy* and traverse low right using undercuts and presses to a long reach right to a distant blunt undercut pinch, then climb the blunt arête of *Tormentil*. No standing on the wee blocs. FA John Watson, 2021.

☐ 5. **Tormentil**          5+

The left side of the blunt arête. Step on the wee blocs and gain a blunt right arête hold. Step up using a left undercling to gain the seam round on the right of the arête, then step up to the big jugs to the top. FA John Watson, 2021.

☐ 6. **Spring Arête** ★          6c

Sit start up the rib above the spring (left of the crack) to the slabby arête. Clever and powerful moves lead into the stand-up finish. FA Lewis Roy, 2020.

☐ 6a. **Spring Holiday**          5+

Stand start to the slabby arête, gaining the cracks on the slabs and the big jug.

☐ 7. **'S No Flake**          6b

Sit start the crack in the join between the two blocs. FA Fraser Harle, 2021.

☐ 8. **Spring Break**          3

Mantle over the bulge right of the crack using undercuts and no crack.

☐ 9. **Sundew**          3+

Mantle over the bulge on the far right with a long reach left to a sprag. A sit start along the handrail to join this is 6b.

## CRIMINAL BLOC >>>

Just left of the Spring Blocs above a good man-made platform.

☐ 1. **Delinquent**          5+

The wall on the left above the step-off flake. Use crimp sidepulls near the crack and no feet in or to the right of the crack.

☐ 2. **Yakuza**          6b

The niche and wall left of the crack without the left arête, feet allowed right of the crack.

☐ 3. **Crack Thief** ★          6a

An excellent problem. Sit start and layback the niche crack on its right side to a barndoor topout. FA Fraser Harle, 2021.

★ *Kev Gibson on Common Assault*

SCHWIG BLOC

THE TOMBSTONE

❏ 4. **The Big Heist**                                        6c
The main wall on the left through slopey holds. No crack holds.
❏ 5. **The Getaway**                                          6c+
A stacked mat or morpho sit start from undercuts on the right through the horizontal break. Finish direct with a scary top-out.
❏ 6. **In Cold Blood** ★                                      6c+
Smear start from undercuts left of the right arête to pounce to the break, then traverse left to a flange and top-out as for *The Big Heist*. FA Kev Gibson, 2021.
❏ 7. **Common Assault**                                       6b
Sit start the arête on the right side of the wall using holds on both sides but keeping left of the arête to the top. FA Kev Gibson, 2021.
❏ 8. **Pick Pocket** ★                                        5
Climb the right sidewall and the arête via sidepulls and pinches to good hidden holds at the top.

## LOWER SPRING BLOCS >>>
Below the Spring Blocs are a few short cleaned blocs on the rocky slope. The first is a roof, the second is a red-veined wall at the very base of the slope.
❏ 1. **Mantle**                                               6b
Mantle over the rounded roof bulge onto the slabby top.
❏ 2. **Red-Eye Left**                                         6b
Sit start and gain the slab's handrail onto the slab.
❏ 2. **Red-Eye**                                              6c
Sit start left but rock right to a mono and use slopers to pull over onto the slab.
❏ 3. **Red-Eye Arête**                                        4
Sit start the right arête, using jugs on the right. An eliminate trending left is 5.

## SCHWIG BLOC >>>
A grooved wall 20m further east with a big ear jug near the top.
❏ 1. **Schwig**                                               5
Traverse from the right to a central finish to a huge jug and mantle.
❏ 2. **Schwig Dyno**                                          6a
The central dyno to the big ear jug.

## THE TOMBSTONE >>>
The narrow leaning wall 100m east of the Spring Blocs.
❏ 1. **Sepulchre**                                            7a+
The left arête of the wall, trending right to a groove and mantle. FA Lewis Roy, 2020.
❏ 2. **Tombstone** ★                                          7a
The intermittent central cracks to the top. Stepping off the flake makes it easier. FA Kev Gibson, 2020.
❏ 3. **Tombstone Sit Start**                                  7a+
Gain the stand-up from a sit start by the left arête. FA Lewis Roy, 2020.

# ☐ THE WHANGIE

★ Colin Lambton on the crux sequence of the Whangie Traverse

## BLOC NOTES >>>

'The Whangie' is an unusual volcanic gorge, or double cliff, in the volcanic geology overlooking Loch Lomond and the Highlands. In summer, it is a very pleasant spot for an evening in the sun as it faces due west. The climbs are notoriously loose but some solid bouldering can be found on the basalt front face of the crag, or on isolated blocs and pinnacles in front of the main face. Traverses are good and straight-ups jump off at the first jugs or ledges.

## TRAVEL >>>

| | | |
|---|---|---|
| Town | >>> | Carbeth |
| Sat Nav | >>> | G63 9QL |
| Parking | >>> | NS 51106 80858 /// sampling.access.called |
| Blocs | >>> | NS 49157 80587 /// racetrack.mixture.fleet |

Go north through Glasgow's northern suburb of Bearsden onto the A809, taking a left through Bearsden at the Canniesburn Toll roundabout. Continue through residential Bearsden to a right turn after 2km onto Stockiemuir Road. Follow this past the ski slope to another roundabout and head straight across past the petrol station into open country. Follow the A809 for 6km past Craigton and Carbeth (cafe), then uphill through forested country to sudden parking on the left at the Queen's View carpark. From here, it is a 2km easy walk west to the cliffs and pinnacles of The Whangie (it's best to wear big boots as it is very boggy). Contour low under the escarpment towards the forestry, where the crag will appear suddenly on the left. A return can be made across the plateau over Auchineden Hill and the trig point.

## SECTORS >>>

❑ **The Gendarme** is the pinnacle just before the ❑ **Main Crag** which is about 12m high and runs N-S for 50m. It has a curious chasm and raised viewpoint at the back of the crag. Its distinctive features are ribbed pinnacles with traditional cracklines on each side. The main crag provides some jump-off straight-ups and traverses of variable lengths. In front of the crag are smaller craglets, including ❑ **Andy's Bloc** just in front of the central main crag, ❑ **Lomond Roof** at the front of the south end, the juggy ❑ **Overhang Bloc** and the ❑ **Hidden Blocs** at the north end in front of the Angel Face of the Gendarme.

## PROBLEMS >>>

❑ 1. **Angel Face** ★         *The Gendarme*     6a
The technical west vertical wall on right of a corner. Crimpy and technical moves allow a lunge for a juggy ledge in the middle of the wall. Jump off or continue boldly through high ledges to traverse off.

❑ 2. **The Porthole**         *Main Crag*     5+
Sit start the left edge of the main crag and use a blunt arête to gain the big 'porthole' pocket, up to jugs on the right of the wall and downclimb a corner.

❑ 3. **Rune Wall**         *Main Crag*     6a+
The leaning main wall of the grassy bay. From SS finger ledges on the right,

# THE WHANGIE

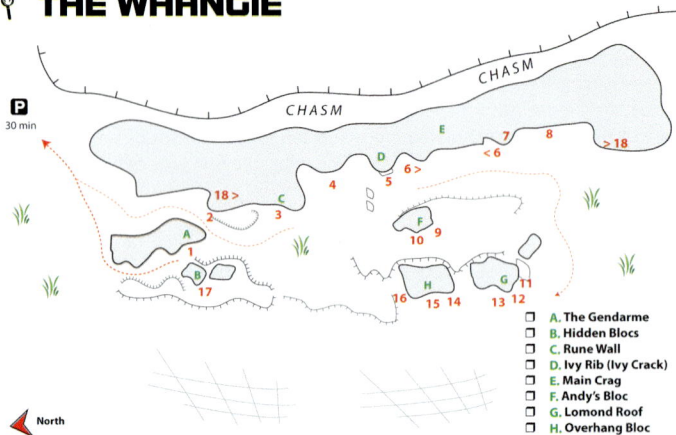

P
30 min

CHASM

CHASM

E

7
8

D
6 >

< 6

> 18

18 >

C

4
5

2
3

A

1

F

10    9

B

17

H

G

16    15    14

13    12    11

North

☐ **A.** The Gendarme
☐ **B.** Hidden Blocs
☐ **C.** Rune Wall
☐ **D.** Ivy Rib (Ivy Crack)
☐ **E.** Main Crag
☐ **F.** Andy's Bloc
☐ **G.** Lomond Roof
☐ **H.** Overhang Bloc

★ *Little Arête*

★ *Angel Face*

★ *Blocks Roof*

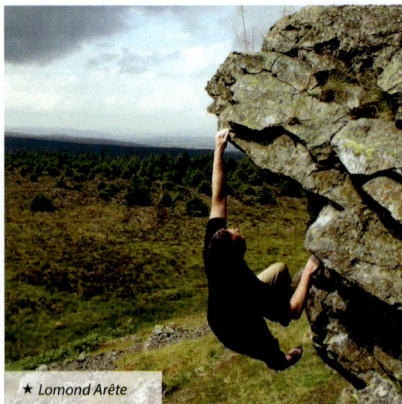

★ *Lomond Arête*

cross through to a sloping hold and twist up and left to ledges, gain a standing position on these to finish.

❒ 4. **Bulge Traverse**          *Main Crag*          6b+

The back of the bay left of the pinnacles has a steep bulge, traverse it from left to right over a low and hard steep section.

❒ 5. **Lego Polisman/Ivy Rib**     *Main Crag*          6b

The pinnacle rib direct between the two cracks (Ivy Crack & Backstep Chimney). From lip slopers, gain hidden holds then crank up to jugs above the bulge, downclimb Backstep.

❒ 6. **Whangie Traverse ★**        *Main Crag*          6c+

Start at ramp jugs just right of Backstep Chimney. A low crux sequence under the bulge gains the next corner, continue low rightwards on blind holds to a hands-off corner at 7.

❒ 7. **Fingaripper**               *Main Crag*          6b

The small hanging slab below Curving Crack (end of traverse). SS on left and use layback slopers to hold on lip, pull over onto short slab via finger slot and gain jugs above.

❒ 8. **Right Wall**                *Main Crag*          5+

Sit start the vertical wall above grass on the far right, using sidepulls up to jump-off jugs.

❒ 9. **Andy's Lip**                *Andy's Bloc*         6a

The wee pinnacled boulder in the scree in front of the traverse has a fun R-L traverse to rock left at the end.

❒ 10. **Andy's Problem**           *Andy's Bloc*         6b

Sit as deep as you can under the roof and gain the crack to rock over directly.

❒ 11. **Lomond Arête**             *Lomond Roof*         5

From jugs, dyno up to a sloping arête and rock over on slabby flanged rock.

❒ 12. **Lomond Groove**            *Lomond Roof*         6a

Sit start the left-hand roof on the front. Gain jugs over the lip and rock up right to the groove.

❒ 13. **Lomond Boys**              *Lomond Roof*         6c

Sit start at holds in the cave and slap up and left through poor holds to a good sequence regaining *Lomond Groove*.

❒ 14. **The Blocks Layback**       *Overhang Bloc*       3+

The blocky laybacking on the right of the roof leads to a highball top out.

❒ 15. **The Blocks Roof**          *Overhang Bloc*       4

The blocky roof can be mantle-shelfed centrally, easier but highish climbing to the top.

❒ 16. **Roof Arête**               *Overhang Bloc*       5+

Climb the left side of the cramped arête and continue directly on the left side.

❒ 17. **Little Arête**             *Hidden Bloc*         6a

Sit start the little arête on the right and climb up left.

❒ 18. **The Full Whangie**         *Main Crag*          7a

A long L-R traverse of the main crag, starting at *The Porthole* and finishing by on ledges at the far right. There are several distinct crux sections and rests.

★ *Mark Dobson on The Art of War*

Craigmore (the 'big crag' in Gaelic) is a north-east facing crag on the northern outskirts of Glasgow. It sits under a blunt ridge of trees on the high ground to the west of Strathblane and commands a terrific view north to the Highlands. Despite being known as a Glasgow crag, officially it sits in the Stirling council ward of Forth & Endrick.

The rock is a dimpled basalt which chalks up to attractive slopers and small crimps. Finger-lock cracks seem to be the key to many problems and routes, as well as good technique with the feet. The British Geological Survey classifies the rock as a volcanic 'plagioclase-macrophyric' basalt of the 'Carbeth Lava Member' formed approximately 331 to 345 million years ago in the Carboniferous Period. As a rock to climb on, it behaves, as John Kerry noted in the 1975 guide, like 'a cross between granite and gritstone'. The basalt at its best gives a satisfying element of subtlety to the boulder problems. However, the shady aspect allows the moss and vegetation to take hold quickly, so problems often have to be brushed or cleaned (carefully).

Despite its shady aspect, it catches glimpses of the summer sun in the morning and evening, at each end of the 200m long crag, which at its highest point reaches about 15m. The crag descends in height towards the northwest to smaller walls and pinnacles. The base of the crag is a dense mixed deciduous forest and home to a rich variety of flora & fauna, so please respect this. Most of the higher problems are traditionally top-roped as many require heavy cleaning before ground-up attempts. Top-rope arrangements are best set up from the bigger trees, though some belays can be made further back from fence posts if necessary. The bouldering feels a little more secure with big mats to help pad sometimes uneven ground.

Craigmore is best in a long dry spell in spring and autumn. It can be very damp and green in winter, and even after summer rain it dries very slowly. It is generally sheltered from both sun and wind, though the leaf canopy can protect the crag from light showers. Avoid the summer midge season unless it is a windy day with the wind from the east or north (it is sheltered from the prevailing westerlies). The best of the bouldering can be completed as a Fontainebleau-like circuit, providing a good work-out on varying styles of problem. The southern section is predominantly bouldering on the main crag buttresses, while the northern section gives dispersed boulders and short walls all the way to the end under the lone Scots Pine. There are plenty of easy problems, but many need dedicated brushing before ascents. The harder problems generally tend to be the cleanest and most attractive.

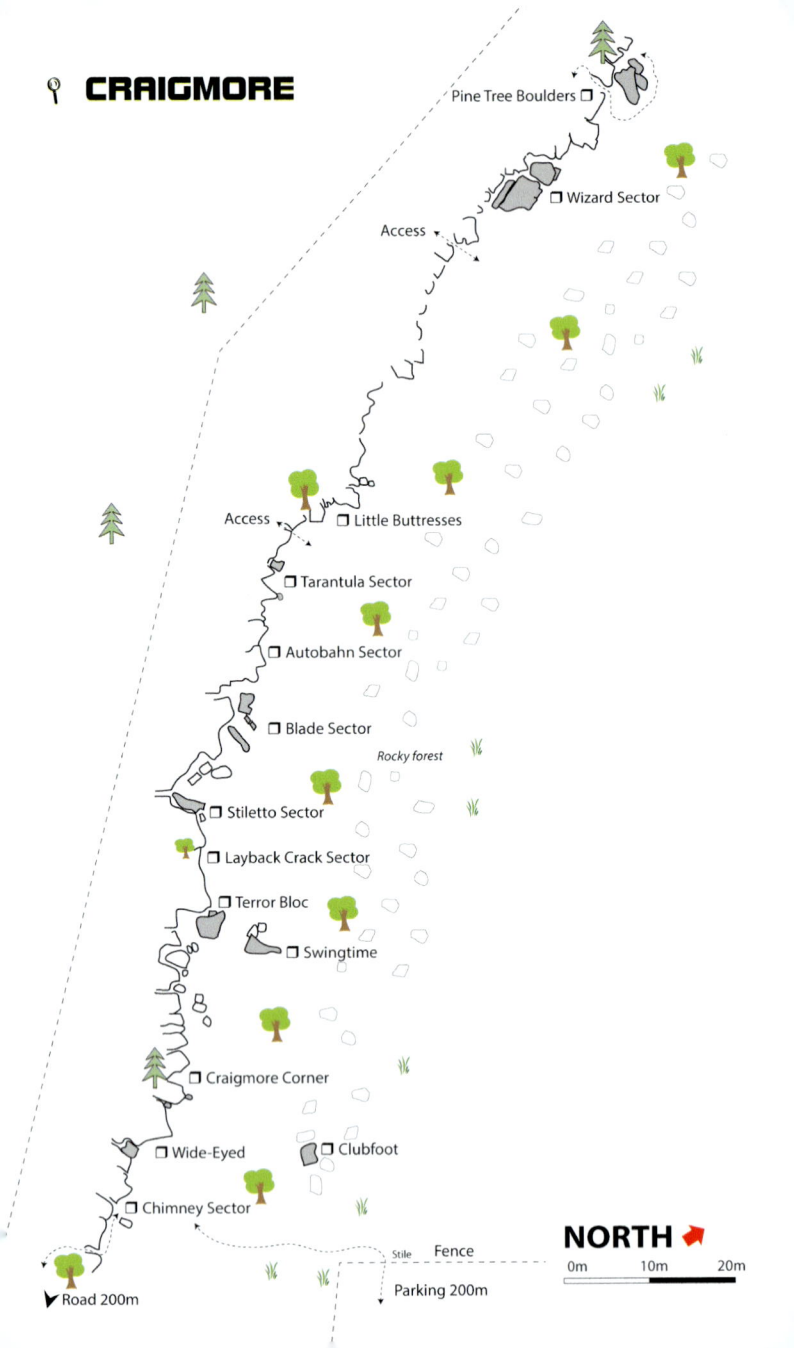

🔍 **CRAIGMORE**

Pine Tree Boulders ☐

☐ Wizard Sector

Access ➤

Access ➤
☐ Little Buttresses

☐ Tarantula Sector

☐ Autobahn Sector

☐ Blade Sector

*Rocky forest*

☐ Stiletto Sector

☐ Layback Crack Sector

☐ Terror Bloc

☐ Swingtime

☐ Craigmore Corner

☐ Wide-Eyed          ☐ Clubfoot

☐ Chimney Sector

Stile   Fence

**NORTH** ➤

0m      10m      20m

➤ Road 200m

↓ Parking 200m

## TRAVEL >>>

| | | |
|---|---|---|
| Town | >>> | Carbeth |
| Sat Nav | >>> | G63 9AS |
| Parking | >>> | NS 52873 79769 /// outcasts.submerge.sweeten |
| Blocs | >>> | NS 62053 89056 /// riverbank.from.pinch |

By car or bike: Craigmore lies to the north of the B821 road, known as Cuilt Brae (a notorious hill climb for cyclists) between Blanefield to the east (on the A81) and Carbeth to the west (on the A809). Take the A809 out of Glasgow through Bearsden into open country past Hilton Park Golf Course to Carbeth, where there's a good cafe. Just after this, take a right turn onto the B821 link road to Strathblane. Continue for 1km past the hut community, through two bends to open fields (big house on the right). Park carefully by the field wall as the road levels out. A stile gives access north to a boggy field and a 200m approach to the crag. Alternatively, walk back up the road (watch out for traffic) and hop a hidden stile onto the tree-lined ridge. Descents to the crag base are 20m before the first pine and halfway along the crag, as well at the last pine at the north end.

Train: from Milngavie train station, follow the signs on the West Highland Way. Walk or bike the West Highland Way to the crag for 5 km, past two lochs to the B821 road junction. Head west on the road, 200m past the re-entrance to the West Highland Way, and hop a stile to fields under the crag (or continue uphill a little opposite the big house to another stile and path up to the ridge-top).

Bus: From Glasgow's Buchanan Street, take the Drymen bus which stops at Milngavie train station and continues on via Carbeth, get off here. Walk north for 200m and turn right onto the B821. Walk along this for 1km through the hutting community to an open field and stile onto the ridge.

## SECTORS >>>

Sectors are described from the distinctive southerly pine tree to the northerly pine tree marking the end of the crag. The first section of vegetated corners is ❑ **Chimney Sector** leading to the cleaner south-east-facing ❑ **Wide-Eyed Wall** with its distinctive crinkle cut cracks. Around the edge of this wall is ❑ **Craigmore Corner** sector, directly under the belay pine. To the right a sequence of trad corners leads to the first separate boulder known as the ❑ **Terror Bloc**. Right of this is the highest wall of Craigmore: ❑ **Layback Crack** under an oak tree. To the right again past the pillar of ❑ **Stiletto** sector leads to ❑ **The Blade** sector right of a separated blade of rock. Right of this is the ❑ **Autobahn Sector** with the slabby walls and high groove of the route *Autobahn*. Going uphill the crag diminishes in height past the boulder walls of the ❑ **Tarantula** sector. The second half of the crag is a sequence of short walls, pinnacles and boulders: ❑ **Little Buttresses** sector, ❑ **The Wizard** sector and the ❑ **Pine Tree Boulders (Jamie's Overhang)** sector.

CHIMNEY SECTOR

CHIMNEY SECTOR R.

## CHIMNEY SECTOR

This is the first sector before the big pine tree on the approach. If approaching via the ridge, drop down a scramble descent 20m before the pine tree. Can be very mossy and green after winter.

❑ 1. **Chimney Arête**                                    3+
The left arête of the cleft-like chimney buttress just right of the mossy slab.

❑ 2. **The Chimney**                                    3+
Climb the awful chimney if you really feel you have to, go left at the top.

❑ 3. **Polo**                                    5+
The short crack on the wall right of *The Chimney*. Most jump off at the break.

❑ 4. **Polover**                                    6a
Takes the right hand crack of the first wee buttress. From two shallow crimps in the break, step up left to the crack and reach high to crozzly holds, then gain the vegetated break with a final highball stretch to the top. Most jump off or downclimb at the first break.

❑ 5. **Tanktop**                                    5+
Eliminate. From small holds in the horizontal break, gain the blunt arête and climb it on its left to join *Silver Arête*.

❑ 6. **Silver Arête**                                    4
Climb the arête on the right, step into and downclimb the corner of *Glug*.

❑ 7. **Glug**                                    2+
The grooved corner right of *Silver Arête,* finish messily or downclimb.

❑ 8. **Grooved Arête**                                    4
The hanging groove right of *Glug*, gain the arête to finish past the tree.

❑ 9. **Totem**                                    6a
Stuck in the corner is a squat pillar boulder with a horizontal midway crack: pull on to this in the centre and gain the sloping jugs at the top with a heel hook. Mantle and downclimb.

❑ 10. **Totem Left**                                    4+
Pull on at the left arête undercut and climb direct to step right to the apex at the top and mantle.

❑ 11. **Totem Left Sit Start**                                    6b
Sit start and slap up to the flat hold then use an undercut and hold in the break just right of the arête to dyno to the top. No bridging. FA Colin Lambton, 2015.

❑ 12. **Totem Sit**                                    6a
Sit start the centre of the bloc, gain the pocket sloper in the break, reach to the left arête, finish via *Totem Left*. FA John Watson, 2015.

❑ 13. **Totem Dyno**                                    6b
Pull on the right-hand pocket undercut and middle undercut, smear on a seam and launch to the high apex jug, hold the swing and mantle, then downclimb.

❑ 14. **Kit Kat**                                    3
The smooth slabbed groove right of the *Totem* block to a ledge and finish up the groove above.

SECTOR WIDE-EYED

★ Colin's Traverse

**SECTOR WIDE-EYED**

❏ 1. **Legless** 6b
The left-hand side of the wall via sidepulls and edges to eventually step off left onto corner ledges or travel right to the high diagonal crack.

❏ 2. **Wide-Eyed** ★ 6c
The highball crinkle-cut crack up the mossy wall. From the snaking vertical crack, lunge to the horizontal break in the centre. Lock-off up on a foot-smearing stretch for reluctant juggy holds, compose and solo or downclimb more easily right. A sit start from low slopers can be contrived.

❏ 3. **Wide-Eyed Direct** 7a
From the horizontal break, use a tiny crimp on the wall to go direct to higher holds in the crack. FA Cameron Bell, 1990s.

❏ 4. **Harmless** 6a
The crack on the right is solved with a fingerlock, with high steps leading to a crossover to a jug, downclimb the niche to the right.

❏ 5. **Harmless Sit Left** 6b
Sit start left of *Harmless*. Use undercuts, very low footholds and a left-hand crack to reach starting holds of *Harmless*. No right arête.

❏ 6. **Wide-Eyed Traverse** 6b+
From the far right of the wall travel low left with tricky moves to cross the first vertical crack, then follow the horizontal break past the second crack to step off at the corner at *Totem*.

❏ 7. **Colin's Traverse** 7a+
Start right of *Harmless* at a sit start and take a very low sequence leftwards, tiptoeing along the lowest footholds just over the grass, past a crux sequence on the middle low wall to finish along a low sequence to *Totem*. Wickedly technical. FA Colin Lambton, 2010.

❏ 8. **Arrowhead Left-Hand** 4
On the right of the wall is a pinnacle – climb the left edge to a niche and ramp. Either solo up ledges to the top, or downclimb the niche.

❏ 9. **Arrowhead Left Bloc** 6b+
Sit start at *Harmless* and climb straight up to a sloper on *Arrowhead Eliminate*, match this and finish up the same. FA Colin Lambton, 2010.

❏ 10. **Arrowhead Right-Hand** 3+
Takes the large crack on the right side of pinnacle.

❏ 11. **Arrowhead Eliminate** 6a
Sit start at the base of *Arrowhead* right crack and climb this to a right-facing pinch. Gain a sloper left of the right-hand crack to gain a high hold above.

❏ 12. **Chimney Traverse** 6b
Sit start at *Harmless*, climb to the break and traverse this left to *Kit Kat*. Trickier than it looks.

❏ 13. **Hi, Low, Off to Totem We Go** 6c
Start up *Chimney Traverse* and follow this to the crack of *Wide-Eyed*, make moves down this to a line of low holds which allows the corner to be passed and the break of *Totem* to be gained, finish up this. FA Colin Lambton, 2010.

★ Merlin

CRAIGMORE CORNER

## CRAIGMORE CORNER SECTOR

□ 1. **Cariad Bloc**                                        5+

The horizontally cracked wall left of the corner to a standing position. Jump off.

□ 2. **Merlin** ★                                           6c

Right of the holly-tree corner is a blunt arête (*The Beast*). Climb the vertical face on the left of this from foot ledges. Use cunning to gain a right-hand crimp, then the crux left-hand pocket. More technique allows a slap up right to jump-off jugs in the narrow corner. FA John Watson, 2007.

□ 3. **The Beast**                                          6a

Right of the holly-tree corner is a blunt arête. Climb up this through the blunt nose to get a footless standing position. Jump off.

□ 4. **Jolly Green Dragon**                                 5+

Gain a standing position on ledges right of *The Beast* and climb off right.

□ 5. **Dolly Jean Dragqueen**                               6b+

This excellent eliminate problem sit-starts at a V-hold down and right, matches the break's crimpy finger-slopers, then telescopes all the way up to a sloping ledge off a left foot smear. Finish standing on a ledge. FA Colin Lambton, 2005.

□ 5a. **Dolly Direct**                                      6c

Eliminate but well worth doing. Sit start at the V-hold, up to the left-hand crimp only, then smear up all the way to the big flat top hold. Reversing down the same problem makes it harder. FA Colin Lambton, 2005.

□ 6. **Tom and Jerry Bloc**                                 5+

The blunt arête between *Tom and Jerry Wall* and *Rampage* crack to a jug at 4m. Downclimb left or right.

□ 6a. **Tom and Jerry Sit Bloc**                            6a

Sit start at the big triangular jugs at the start of *T&J Wall*, move right round the corner to gain the arête and rock up left on a foot jug to the big niche jug.

□ 6b. **Tom and Jerry Eliminate**                           6c+

Sit start *Tom and Jerry* by the left corner, go right to the blunt arête. Climb this via a right-hand arête pinch and a left-hand sloper only to high vertical slots which are infuriating to hold (no jugs out right). Finish at jugs above.

## TERROR BLOC SECTOR

□ 1. **Terror Left**                                        4+

Climb the left face of the *Terror* boulder using jugs and the arête to reach up left to slopers, then mantle direct onto the top.

□ 2. **Terror** ★                                           5+

Puzzles even the most experienced of locals. Gain good incut slots on the hanging arête, pull hard and step up on the arête via smears. Lock off to a high crack hold and get stood up, then mantle over on the right.

□ 3. **Terror Sit Start**                                   6c

A bunched and cramped sit start with a left hand in an undercut low on the left wall and a right hand on a poor arête pinch, then slap for the arête finger jugs and finish up the stand-up version. A harder original version at 7a was climbed with a left hand on the arête and a desperate pull to the jugs.

TERROR BLOC

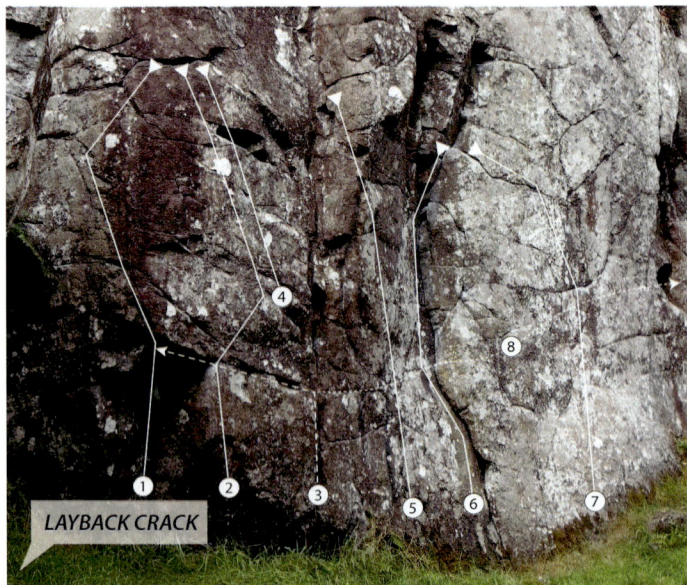

LAYBACK CRACK

☐ 4. **Terror Right**                                          6b+

The right-hand face. From the big slot and the flat hold on the arête, smear up and gain the high crack crimp with the left hand, then a right-hand crimp on the face allows a steep pull to the vertical right crack and the top.

☐ 4a. **Terror Right Sit Start**                               6c+

Sit start as for *Terror Sit Start* but transition right to the slot and up *Terror Right*.

☐ 5. **Confusion**                                             6a+

A good problem. Sit start laybacking the niche corner crack and bridge up to get stood under the wall right of *Terror*. From here, take the slot with the left hand and use a blunt right undercut pinch to step up to stand on the ledge. Slap or the lip and mantle out. FA John Watson, 2020.

## LAYBACK CRACK SECTOR

☐ 1. **Andy's Arête** ★                                        6c+

The arête left just opposite the *Terror* bloc on the crag. Sit start with a clever sequence from the wee niche pinch and undercut. Gain smooth crimps above, stretch up left to a poor jam/crimp then levitate up and right to the letterbox jugs. Some use a right undercut on the wall. FA Andy Gallagher, 1980s.

☐ 2. **Andy's Wall**                                           6c

The wall direct just right of the left arête. Sit start at left and right sidepulls. Pull up to a slopey right-hand hold, gain the left-hand triangle crimp common to *Andy's Arête*, then lock up to a triangular sloper. From here, snatch to the slopey ledge, match carefully and gain the higher letterbox. Jump off.

☐ 3. **Andy's Link**                                           7a

Sit start on the right and traverse low to join the arête, using the crap sloper, no other jugs above. FA Colin Lambton, 2013.

☐ 4. **Stand-Up Routine**                                      6b+

Winter sloper eliminate! Use the left triangle and a big right sloper common to *Andy's Wall* to step on and deadpoint to the letterbox sloper with a left hand. Match the slopers and udge desperately for the jugs above. No big sidepull in the letterbox. FA John Watson, c2005.

☐ 5. **Left-Hand Wall**                                        6a+

Wall left of *Layback Crack*. Start at a sidepull, gain edges on a shield feature and climb up left to a good hold. No holds in the crack or left arête. Slightly eliminate but worthwhile.

☐ 6. **Layback Crack**                                         3+

Climb the crack to a big jug at 5m, downclimb and jump off.

☐ 7. **Layback Wall Bloc**                                     6c

The wall just right of *Layback Crack* (holds in this are out of bounds). Tiptoe up direct using a crux right pocket and left sidepulls to snap for a right-hand finger jug and traverse left to the jug in the corner. Downclimb. Don't veer too far right or high into *Craig's Wall*! FA John Watson, 2013.

☐ 8. **Layback Crack Traverse**                                6b

The crag can be traversed at a low level from a sit-start at the left arête to finish at the corner left of *Samson*. Technical and fingery after the crack.

STILETTO SECTOR

BLADE SECTOR

## STILETTO SECTOR

These are usually jumped off or downclimbed after the initial difficulties.

☐ 1. **Samson Left**                                             6a

Sit start sidepulls on the left wall, gain a left sloper in the groove, rock up on a left foot to throw a right hand to the V-groove common to *Samson*. No jugs.

☐ 2. **Samson Bloc ★**                                      6b+

The short blank wall above an embedded stone left of the distinctive curving crack and pillar. Pull on with a poor left undercut to rock onto a sketchy left foot edge and wobble powerfully left to match a V-groove. Jump off from jugs.

☐ 3. **Sgian Dubh**                                              6a

A stand start taking on the hanging arête feature in between the cracks of *Stiletto* and *Sabre* directly. No bridging. Almost certainly climbed before, but a worthwhile eliminate with good balancy climbing.

☐ 4. **Scabbard Traverse**                                 4+

Sit start hard right under the *Stiletto* pillar, gain the crack round the corner, then traverse up and left via the wee hanging arête to high jugs on *Sabre Crack*, step off onto the wee block. Good warm up.

☐ 5. **Triplets Traverse**                                    5+

Small set of triplet blocs jammed together right of *Stiletto*. May need cleaned. Sit start on the far right and traverse the ledges to the left.

☐ 6. **Triplets Low Traverse**                            6c

Eliminate sit start right-to-left traverse.  Painful jams, long stretches and a masochism to ignore the most blatant ledge holds. Just sidepulls and jams only to a crux crossover to arête holds. FA Colin Lambton, March 2015.

## BLADE SECTOR

☐ 1. **The Blade**                                                  5

Under a high wall sits a detached slabby blade of rock. Usually moss-covered.

☐ 2. **Tae a Moose Bloc Sit**                             5+

Two wee walls under *The Blade*. Sit start up right to the arête and up.

☐ 3. **Tae a Moose Bloc**                                    2+

Take the crack splitting the two small walls.

☐ 4. **Latch Key Kid ★**                                     6c+

Step on with a low right-hand undercut pinch (no crack) and gain a sharp left-hand crimp, then dyno up to jugs. To be done matless. FA John Watson, 1999.

☐ 5. **Tic Tac**                                                        5

The right wall using only the rib on the right.

## AUTOBAHN SECTOR

☐ 1. **Stoater**                                                       5+

The blunt arête forming the left edge of the niche. Use poor slopers to balance up to a juggy break and higher ledges, traverse left or right and downclimb.

☐ 2. **Autobahn Bloc**                                        6a+

The wall right of the corner taken direct. Climb from the slot via tiny crimps and sidepulls up to better holds and ledges, traverse off right.

AUTOBAHN SECTOR

TARANTULA SECTOR

☐ 3. **All Hope**      4
The crack on the right of the wall leads to ledges, downclimb right.
☐ 4. **Hendo's Obsession**      5+
The arête right of the crack to join *All Hope* route.
☐ 5. **Hendo's Sit Start**      6a
Sit start at the stepped niche under the right arête. Traverse up and right to holds round the corner, then gain the arête of *Hendo's* and finish up this.
☐ 6. **Elk**      3
The mossy corner next right may need a good clean.
☐ 7. **Ell**      4
The cracked wall to the right again may be very dirty.

## TARANTULA SECTOR
☐ 1. **Tarantula**      5
Right of *Ell* is a bulge above a scoop. Climb to hidden jugs on the nose, pull over and finish up the groove. Highball.
☐ 2. **Leech Arête Left**      7a
Start on the *Tarantula* side. Climb into the scoop using poor slopey holds on the arête. Gain the slopey flange holds above to help pull up to gain the *Tarantula* groove. Finish more easily up the highball arête.
☐ 3. **Leech Arête Right**      6c+
Technical moves stepping left up the blunt arête from the ramp of *Leech Direct*.
☐ 4. **Leech Direct ★**      6a
The horizontally cracked wall over a ramp. Climb trending slightly left to a long reach to a ledge and finish direct. Careful, or you are trampolined off the ramp!
☐ 5. **Leech**      5
The cracked wall to traverse left at the high break to rejoin the direct.
☐ 6. **Eel**      4
The wee corner has a tricky finish.
☐ 7. **Coal Face**      3+
The cracked wall right of *Eel*.
☐ 8. **Charcoal Chimney**      3+
The chimney.
☐ 9. **Black Beauty**      4+
The crack right of the chimney, enjoyable climbing.
☐ 10. **Black Power**      3+
The arête right of *Black Beauty*.
☐ 11. **Mat Black**      3
The wall just right of the arête.

## LITTLE BUTTRESSES
☐ 1. **East Wall**      3
Just after the midway descent corner, climb the pinnacle on the left.
☐ 2. **Pinnacle Wall**      3
Climb the highball face of the pinnacle buttress, left of the cracks.

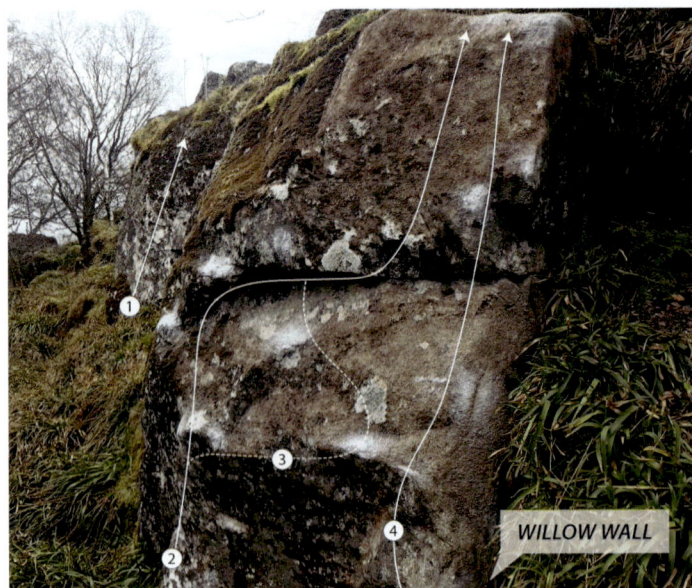

LITTLE BUTTRESSES

WILLOW WALL

☐ 3. **Donald Duck**                                3
The left-hand crack.
☐ 4. **Mickey Mouse**                               3
The right-hand jam crack.
☐ 5. **Piglet**                                     3
The wall just right of *Mickey Mouse*.
☐ 6. **Pig's Ear**                                  4
Up *Piglet* then right to the arête.
☐ 7. **Silk Purse**                                 4+
The arête to finish up a slab, needs a good clean.
☐ 8. **West Wall**                                  4+
The wall right of *Silk Purse*, tricky moves onto slab. Needs cleaned first.
☐ 9. **Extrarête**                                  5
20m rightwards is a small pinnacle. Take the shallow groove in the arête, finishing up the right. FA Pete Murray, 1990s.
☐ 10. **Sunshine Arête**                            4+
Right of *Extrarête*, step onto the ledge under the wall, then pull into the left groove and step out left to the arête to finish.
☐ 11. **Sunshine Arête Wall**                       4+
The wall right of *Extrarête*. May need a good scrub.

## WILLOW WALL SECTOR

A short attractive wave of rock when cleaned, 10m left of *The Wizard* sector just under the crag lip under a small willow tree.

☐ 1. **Red Wall**                                   6a
20m further right and just left of *Willow Wall* is a reddish wall, usually heavily vegetated. When clean it gives a good short traverse right from a ramp.
☐ 2. **Willow Wall**                                5+
Start from low left on the wall, at the blunt groove/arête. Use a blunt left pinch and right crimp to pull up to a slopey finger-ledge. Shift feet up and right then use a double sidepull to reach right to holds on the arête of *Bumblebee*, step up and finish direct up the wall. FA John Watson, 2019.
☐ 3. **Andy's Problem** ★                           6c
The slopey bulge and wall from a sit start, left hand on sidepull and right on a low sloper. Gain a poor sloper on the right then crank up left to the finger-ledge and surmount the bulge, finish right as for *Willow Wall*. FA Andy Gallagher, 1990s.
☐ 4. **Bumblebee**                                  6a+
The right arête of *Andy's Problem*. Start with a left hand on the big sidepull out left and right hand on a sidepull right of the arête. Pull on and smear up feet. Gain a left press on the vertical feature up and left, then snatch right for sidepulls on the arête. Use these in an odd sequence to get established on the wall, finish with a mantle. FA John Watson, 2019.

WIZARD SECTOR

★ Andy Gallagher topping out The Wizard

The amphitheatre of slabs, pillars, and walls towards the end of the crag, centred by the distinctive high pillar of *The Wizard*.

❐ 1. **Rowan Tree Wall**                                    5+
Just before *The Wizard* sector, there is a short wall under a small rowan tree, which turns the corner onto the cracked slabs. Climb up the wall direct from the horizontal break. Technical and fingery. Eliminate arête.

❐ 2. **Left Arête**                                         3+
Pull up over the bulge on jugs to get stood on the horizontal break of *Rowan Tree Wall*. Climb the arête until you can turn the arête on the right near the top. Finish up the slab.

❐ 3. **Cracked Slab**                                       3
The toed, cracked slab left of *The Wizard* has various vegetated problems.Climb the big crack splitting the slab, take the right crack to finish up the wall.

❐ 4. **The Slab**                                           3
Climb cracks in the slab right of *Cracked Slab*. Finish up the wall above.

❐ 5. **Elephant Foot**                                      6a
Sit start the cracked slab at the base of the crack, a heel in the niche, aiming for slopers just right of the crack, then mantle onto the slab, finish up this.

❐ 6. **Elephant Foot Traverse**                             6a+
Sit start as for *Elephant Foot* but traverse low left round the corner without the high break to finish up *Rowan Tree Wall*. Eliminate.

❐ 7. **Right Arête**                                        6b
Sit start and pull onto the right edge of the cracked slab. Finish easily.

❐ 8. **Cave Route**                                         2
Just right of the slab is a dirty caved chimney.  Climb it if you must!

❐ 9. **Slab Traverse**                                      3
From *Tree Wall* gain the arête, traverse right across the slab to *Right Arête* and finish up this.

❐ 10. **The Wizard** ★                                      6b+
This conical highball boulder looks like Gandalf's hat. Its main arête has a hard and technical start and can be escaped at half height but purists will want to finish it direct.  The top requires a steady and confident approach.

❐ 11. **Wizard Sit Start**                                  7a
Sit start in the wee cave at a slot and wee arête hold on the right. Pull up to gain the sidepull on the left arête and lunge up and right for a poor finger sloper, then join the main problem. Finish it to the top.

❐ 12. **Wizard Sit Start Eliminate**                        7b+
A desperate eliminate of the sit start, using only the left arête holds from the low slots start (no wee arête out right, nor the finger sloper up and right). Very powerful and barndoory. FA Paul Savage, 1990s.

❐ 13. **Wight Wizard**                                      6a
Sit start the right niche to climb the arête using crimps and smears to a half-height jug, keep going direct on the left to an airy top. No escaping early right.

★ Suzy P

SUZY Q SECTOR

⑭ ⑮ ⑯ ⑰ ⑱ ⑲ ⑳ ㉑

❐ 13a. **Tarot**                                    2+

The right slabs of *The Wizard* pinnacle. Tiptoe up right to ledges to an easy top.

❐ 14. **Suzy P**                                    6b

The narrow pillar 4m right of *The Wizard* bloc. Sit start the left side of the arête, bearhugging up the narrow wall to the top. FA John Watson, 2021.

❐ 15. **Suzy Q ★**                                  5

A puzzling stand start up the cracked wall, using the ledge and crack. Mantle onto the ledge and take the crack to the top trending left.

❐ 16. **Suzy R**                                    6a

The wall right of the crack, without using the arête and the good ledge. Use the crack and wall holds to a reach left to a hold under the tree at the top. FA John Watson, 2021.

❐ 17. **Victory V**                                 4

The diagonal crack in the roofed buttress 7m to the right of *The Wizard* gives a short overhang problem pulling right of the crack. No standing on blocks in the chimney.

❐ 18. **Victory V Eliminate**                       6a

Eliminate sit start left from the niche up the hanging arête – no bridging.

❐ 19. **Wopitee**                                   5+

Bold. Start under the roofed niche to the right of *Victory V*. Bridge up to gain the wall above the roof, then pull over boldly to the top ledge.

❐ 20. **Expo**                                      6a

Climb the arête under the roof and pull over to the top. Bold and committing, needs a few mats and a confident approach.

❐ 21. **Two Tree Wall**                             4

The arête and the right wall to an exposed step left at the top.

❐ 22. **Toad**                                      3+

The crack below and right of *Two Tree Wall* to a ledge. Finish up the wall above.

❐ 23. **Rizla**                                     3

The short mossy wall on the right of *Toad*.

❐ 24. **Amphitheatre Girdle**                       5

The full traverse of the bay from the short wall right of *Tarot*, crossing *Suzy Q* to below the roof of *Wopitee* (crux), then round the corner and finish up *Rizla*.

## PINE TREE SECTOR (JAMIE'S OVERHANG)

The leaning pillar bloc under the pine tree at the end of the crag. It has a slabby side and a short overhanging side, surrounded by small walls.

❐ 1. **Pine Cone Slab**                             2

The slabby back of *Jamie's Overhang*. Take the slab at its easiest. Usually needs a good clean.

❐ 2. **Terminal Arête**                             4+

The back of Jamie's Overhang (downhill side) has a slabbed arête, taken from its steeper right side, then rock left round onto the slab.

❐ 2a. **Terminal Arête 'All In'**                   6b

Sit start with both feet on the pedestal under the overhang. Move straight up

JAMIE'S OVERHANG

★ *Colin Lambton on Chop Phooey*

to gain the arête and then keep on the steeper face to the top. The vertical cracks on the slab are in, as is the right arête.

☐ 2b. **No Forking Crack**        6b+

Sit start but don't move left and stick to the steeper side, up the face to the top over a poor landing. The cracks on the slab are out.

☐ 2c. **Dress to the Left**        6c+

Sit start with both feet on the pedestal under the overhang. The cracks on the slab face are in, but the right hand corner holds are out. The landing needs careful protection. FA Jamie Taylor, 2021.

☐ 2d. **Keep It Clean**        7b

Sit start and use smears to stand up, without using either arête, to gain the first break. Use the bottom part of the bifurcated crack to layaway and gain the good hold below the second break and the top. FA Jamie Taylor, 2021.

☐ 3. **Jamie's Overhang** ★        6a

Stand start with left hand on the apex sloper and right on a lower right sloper by the corner. Pull on and gain a very sharp right-hand crimp on the slab to mantle over the roof to a long left scar, usually unhelpfully filled with pine straw. FA Jamie Taylor, 1980s.

☐ 4. **Jamie's Traverse**        6a+

Traverse the lip of *Jamie's Overhang,* from a sit start *a cheval* on the prop bloc. Gain the lip and slap right to finish via the crimp rockover.

☐ 5. **Jamie's Overhang Left**        6b

From the sinker jugs on the left arête, pull on and gain a poor right-hand finger-sloper on the slab left of the apex. Choose footholds carefully and slap for the scar and mantle onto the slab.

☐ 6. **Jamie's Overhang Sit**        6b+

AKA 'Nice Guys Finish Last'. From the cave's crimpy break, snatch almost footless for the good left flattie, heel-hook left and slap up right to the sloper right of apex, gain the sharp right-hand crimp to the slab rockover. FA 1990s.

☐ 7. **Jamie's Overhang Eliminate**        6c

Basically *Jamie's Overhang* sit start without the heel-hook.

☐ 8. **The Art of War** ★        6c+

Essentially an eliminate direct of *Jamie's Overhang Sit*. From the twin crimps, slap right to the far right sloper by the arête and pull over via the crimp. Climbed in the 90s by Paul Savage, Andy Gallagher, John Watson, Colin Lambton and sometimes called the *Sun Tzu Dyno,* just to add to the confusion!

☐ 9. **Monkey Hanger**        7a

As for *Jamie's Overhang Sit*, gain the good left hold, but use no heels out left. Smear on and boost far right to the fat sloper on the arête. Match this (usually footless), then mantle via the sharp crimp. Hard to keep your feet off your mats and the rock behind. FA Colin Lambton, 2011.

☐ 10. **Sanjuro**        7a

Sit start at the cave arête hold for right hand, left in the split crimp. Drop into the central sloper hold, then gain the flat hold up left, match this and go up left for the arête jug, then finish as for *Jamie's Left*. FA Paul Savage, 1990s.

PINE TREE BLOCS

★ Jamie's Traverse

**□ 11. Chop Phooey**      6c

Sit start the cave's cramped right arête, left hand out on crimp, right on arête flattie, and slap up to the fat sloper, rockover via the crimp as for the original stand-up. FA Colin Lambton, 2013.

**□ 12. Jamie's Superlow**      7a

Sit start very low with right toe on low edge, left hand in the 'Vulcan' crimp, right hand very low on sloper at the base of the right arête. Pull on to slap right hand into the break and then boost into *The Art of War*.

**□ 13. Surprise Attack**      7b

Sit start the central crimps and dyno direct to the sloping lip just right of the apex (no fat sloper on right) and rock over. Cold conditions and patience are required to reach the sloper and then hang it. FA Dave MacLeod, 1990s.

**□ 14. The Bridge**      4

Sit start in the deep corner under the fat sloper, feet on block, layback off jugs on the right wall backwards to the fat sloper, then bridge up the corner (no big foot ledge) to mantle onto the slab.

**□ 15. Vanguard**      4+

Takes the narrow wall squeezed in between *Jamie's Overhang* and *Pine Cone Wall*. No bridging. Eliminating the foot ledge makes it 5+ (match the flat hold and boost).

**□ 16. Pine Cone Wall**      6a

Just under the pine, this vertical wall is climbed as an eliminate through the sharp crimps to a long stretch to the break. No arête. A crouch or sit start makes it a little harder.

**□ 17. Sunshine Arête**      3

Climb the blunt wee arête under the Scots pine direct. A version on its left side is a little harder.

**□ 18. The Slopester**      3+

Pull on centrally, snap left to the slopey left arête and climb this to top, nice!

**□ 19. Sunburn**      2

The blocky ledges right of *Sunshine Arête* taken on the left-hand side.

## FOREST BOULDERS

Two boulders in the woods below the crag. **□ Clubfoot Bloc** – the triangular overhang at the base of the field below *Wide-Eyed* sector and **□ Swingtime Bloc** – a well-hidden cave lip directly below the *Terror* bloc.

## CLUBFOOT BLOC

**□ 1. Clubfoot Left**      5

Sit start the cramped left arête in the pit, smear on and use jugs to gain the sloping lip, travel right up this a bit and mantle left. FA J Watson, 2017.

**□ 2. Clubfoot Direct**      6a+

An unusual wee problem. Sit start the ledge and heel/toe out right, but cross a right hand up left to a flat lip sloper, then mantle the apex on its left side.

CLUBFOOT BLOC

★ John Watson on Swingtime

❐ **3. Clubfoot**                                           6a

Sit start the right arête. There are two methods: one with a heel-toe; another with an undercut, both allow the arête to be climbed to mantle the apex.

## SWINGTIME BLOC

❐ **1. Swingtime** ★                                        6a+

A left to right lip traverse on the low cave boulder hidden below *Terror,* mantle on the right via the blunt arête to finish.

❐ **2. Ragtime**                                            6c+

Crouch start below the finish of *Swingtime*, left hand in a slot, right hand on a poor sloper. Jam a foot in low right and slap for a right-hand crimp, then again for the lip, cut loose (no brushing mats) and mantle the lip on the right. FA John Watson & Colin Lambton c 2000.

★ *Mark Dobson on Ragtime*

# ❏ TIGER WALLS

TIGER WALL

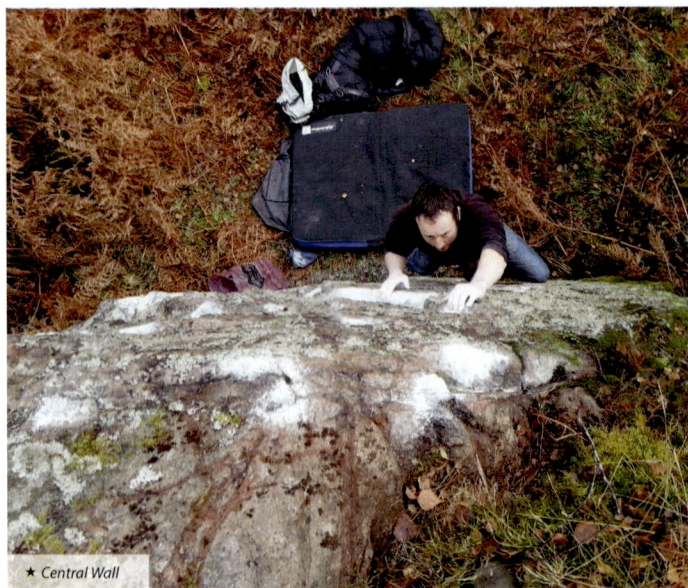

★ Central Wall

## BLOC NOTES >>>

Two red-striped walls about 1km north of Craigmore, but they are best accessed form the nearby Queen's View carpark, which is used as access for The Whangie. They are of the same basaltic rock and provide a few good problems in a pleasant spot of solitude.

## TRAVEL >>>

| Town | >>> | Carbeth |
|------|-----|---------|
| Sat Nav | >>> | G63 9QL |
| Parking | >>> | NS 51106 80858 /// sampling.access.called |
| Blocs | >>> | NS 51407 80751 /// teamed.grab.pedicure |

About 8km north of Bearsden and Milngavie on the A809, park at the Queen's View carpark. The two walls lie about 250m east of the road, facing the Campsie hills across Strathblane. Cross the road carefully, opposite the signpost to Queen's View, hop the fence and welly-walk straight towards a distant stand of pines. The walls appear facing east and south of hillocks after a small valley.
❑ **South Wall** is the short south aspect wall and ❑ **Tiger Wall** sits a bit further north-east under a tree.

## THE PROBLEMS >>>

❑ 1. **South Wall**      *South Wall*      4+
Sit start on the right break, with deceptive moves to gain a standing position.

❑ 2. **Central Wall**      *South Wall*      6b
Sit start the slot and gain the central rail to top out left. FA Colin Lambton, 2013.

❑ 3. **Left Arête**      *Tiger Wall*      5+
The sloping left arête is very good. Climb it to the top and mantle the ledge.

❑ 4. **Tiger Wall**      *Tiger Wall*      6b+
This is the red-striped wall, climbed centrally via a central stand start at crimps. Gain a left-hand pinch and then a poor right sloper, then crimp direct to the top. Using a higher right sloper may reduce the grade a bit.

❑ 5. **Tiger Wall Sit Start**      *Tiger Wall*      6c+ ★
Sit start on the right at sloping jugs, gain a left-hand hold and right crimp under the overlap, travel up left to a poor left crimp and slap for a crux right sloper, then up left to a crimp and a final long reach to the top ledge. Some gaston the crimp. FA John Watson, 2013.

❑ 6. **Entanglement**      *Tiger Wall*      5+
Sit start the groove on the right, via good sidepulls then lovely slopers to the top. Holds out left are allowed.

# GARLOCH ROCKS

MAIN EDGE

STINGRAY BLOC

## BLOC NOTES >>>

This small sandstone venue gives a few walls and blocs facing north-west and are part of 'The Garlochs' outcrops on Garloch hill just north-east of the distinctive volcanic plug of Dumgoyne Hill (which gives its name to the distillery down below). They are best in summer and tend to catch a breeze. The steep approach may put some off, but the rock quality is good and it's a nice esoteric spot. The boulders were discovered and climbed by Andy Gallagher, but undocumented until Rory Harper added names and grades in 2020.

## TRAVEL >>>

| Town | >>> | Strathblane |
| Sat Nav | >>> | G63 9LB |
| Parking | >>> | NS 52788 82501 /// negotiators.earlobe.gadgets |
| Blocs | >>> | NS 54999 83402 /// shimmered.shatters.headlight |

Access is from a small layby just south of the distillery by the forest edge or a larger layby just north of the distillery. Cross a stile into the steep fields and follow the Dumgoyne trail uphill and over a fence. Continue uphill steeply left past Dumgoyne and continue up left on a farm trail to shieling ruins and then contour north to the walls and boulders. A forty-minute leg-buster! ❑ **The Main Edge** is the main event, with a small roof bloc 50m north called ❑ **The Stingray Bloc**. More esoterica can be found below on ❑ **Cuckoo Rock** near the stream, and further north past a sandstone jumble is ❑ **Skinhead Slab**.

## THE PROBLEMS >>>

❑ 1. **Desperate Measures**    *The Main Edge*    6a
At the left end of the main crag, sit start the faint arête and sidepull to gain a cut-out and pocket, then climb up and left. A stand start is 5+.

❑ 2. **The Road to Nowhere** ★    *The Main Edge*    6a+
Traverse from the start of *The Parent Trap* to finish up *Desperate Measures*.

❑ 3. **The Parent Trap**    *The Main Edge*    3
Climb the central groove/corner feature.

❑ 4. **Wingspan**    *The Main Edge*    4
Climb out from the roof from a large undercling to finish on the jug at the lip. Don't touch the wall to the right.

❑ 5. **Punter's Crack**    *The Main Edge*    5
From *Wingspan*, join the hand crack to finish on the jammed block.

❑ 6. **Two Left Feet**    *The Main Edge*    5
Sit start the crack left of *Dancing Queen* and join Dancing Queen to finish.

❑ 7. **Dancing Queen**    *The Main Edge*    6a
Sit start with both hands on the flake and climb the right end of the crag via the thin crack and holds to the right. A stand start is 5.

❑ 1. **Dignity and Grace**    *Stingray Bloc*    5+
Sit start below the jutting roof, slap over to the right and flop onto the top. The little slab underneath is in.

# ☐ STRONEND BLOC

★ *Shotgun Direct*

STRONEND BLOC

## BLOC NOTES >>>

Okay, it's nearer to Stirling, but just within range for a Glasgow day out. This sandstone bloc sits high above Fintry on its northern hills under a crag called Skiddaw, under the hill called Stronend. The rock quality is a little sandy ,but the boulder sits in a picturesque position and has some good problems despite the steep walk. It was opened by Stuart Burns and David Crawford from 2006 to 2009. The boulder can be seen on the skyline on the Kippen to Fintry road.

## TRAVEL >>>

| Town | >>> | Fintry |
|------|-----|--------|
| Sat Nav | >>> | G63 0LS |
| Parking | >>> | NS 61094 88613 /// strumming.horn.televise |
| Blocs | >>> | NS 62053 89056 /// riverbank.from.pinch |

Fintry is a village on the north side of the Campsies accessed via the A81 north of Glasgow and the B818 east after the Dumgoyne distillery. In Fintry take the B822 north signed to Kippen for a mile to park carefully just past the entrance to Balgair Caravan Park. Gain the fields and head uphill between the plantations. On clearing the woods, veer up left steeply to the crag and the boulder below, about 30 minutes puffing.

## THE PROBLEMS >>>

❒ 1. **Pockets Roof**                6a
North wall. Stand start to wall below the roof using pockets to mantle.

❒ 2. **Roof Sitter**                6b
Sit start under the north roof and use undercut to gain roof.

❒ 3. **Stronend Wall**                6b
Undercut the corner of the roof to a crimp and gain the wall to mantle over the top.

❒ 4. **Balducci's Mantle ★**                6b
Gain the slopey ledge to match a high hold and mantle over the top. The original problem is from the crimps on the mantle direct up to the high hold. Using a crimp out right reduces the grade to 6a. FA Stuart Burns, 2009.

❒ 5. **Ambulo**                6a+
Crouch start by the west roof and traverse right along crack to a right mantle.

❒ 6. **Shotgun Arête**                5
The grooved right arête to move left at the top. A direct finish is 5+.

❒ 7. **Shotgun Direct**                6a+
Sit start the right arête and trend up the right side to a slopey top-out.

❒ 8. **Pocket Wall**                3
South face. Pockets on the left to a mantle.

❒ 9. **Double Pockets**                4
South face. Central line through the big pockets.

❒ 10. **Buchaille's Big Day Out**                3
The right side of the south face.

# MUGDOCK

MUGDOCK WALL

## MUGDOCK WALL

| Town | >>> | Strathblane (Mugdock) |
| Sat Nav | >>> | G62 8EJ |
| Parking | >>> | NS 55758 77483 /// lousy.trickle.jetliner |

This outcrop offers a small bouldering option right opposite the Mugdock East carpark. A slightly overhanging wall trends right to a slabbier wall. Landings are good though top-outs are quite vegetated. FAs by Jack McKechnie in 2015.

❏ **1. Warm-Up**                                              5
Start at the left-hand side of the wall, move up to the jug and then top out.
❏ **2. Pssh Easy**                                          6a+
Start in the crack up to a juggy sidepull between the layaway for *Unexpected* and the jug for the *Warm-Up* route.
❏ **3. Unexpected**                                          6b
Sit start into the crack and gain a right-hand incut. Move up to a left-hand layaway crimp and dyno for a jug with the right. Top out right.
❏ **4. Undercuts**                                          5+
Next to the descent route, there is a bulge. Undercut this, move right and up.
❏ **5. Gully**                                              5+
Climb the gully to the right of the main wall.
❏ **6. Descent Route**                                       2
The far-right route is a good descent.

★ *Cameron Bell in the 1980s on Craigmore's Wide-Eyed*

# ◻ CRAIGMADDIE

### INTRODUCTION >>>

Craigmaddie is a sandstone bouldering venue on the moors north-east of Milngavie. A band of variable conglomerate/sandstone runs west to east along the moors underneath the volcanic spillages of the Kilpatrick hills and the Campsies. In general, it outcrops as a scrittly and pocketed sandstone, but in its more compact sectors it is almost like gritstone. The best concentration of bouldering is on 'Craigmaddie Muir' above the Mugdock reservoirs, around the glacial erratic pile of the Auld Wives' Lifts (no climbing on the historical carvings). It has been a quiet bouldering spot for years and was originally climbed on in the 1990s by Willie Gorman, who climbed some longer crag-style routes but never recorded anything. It then saw more local attention in the 2000s. The elevated southerly outlook of the crag takes in the whole glory of Glasgow and the Clyde estuary.

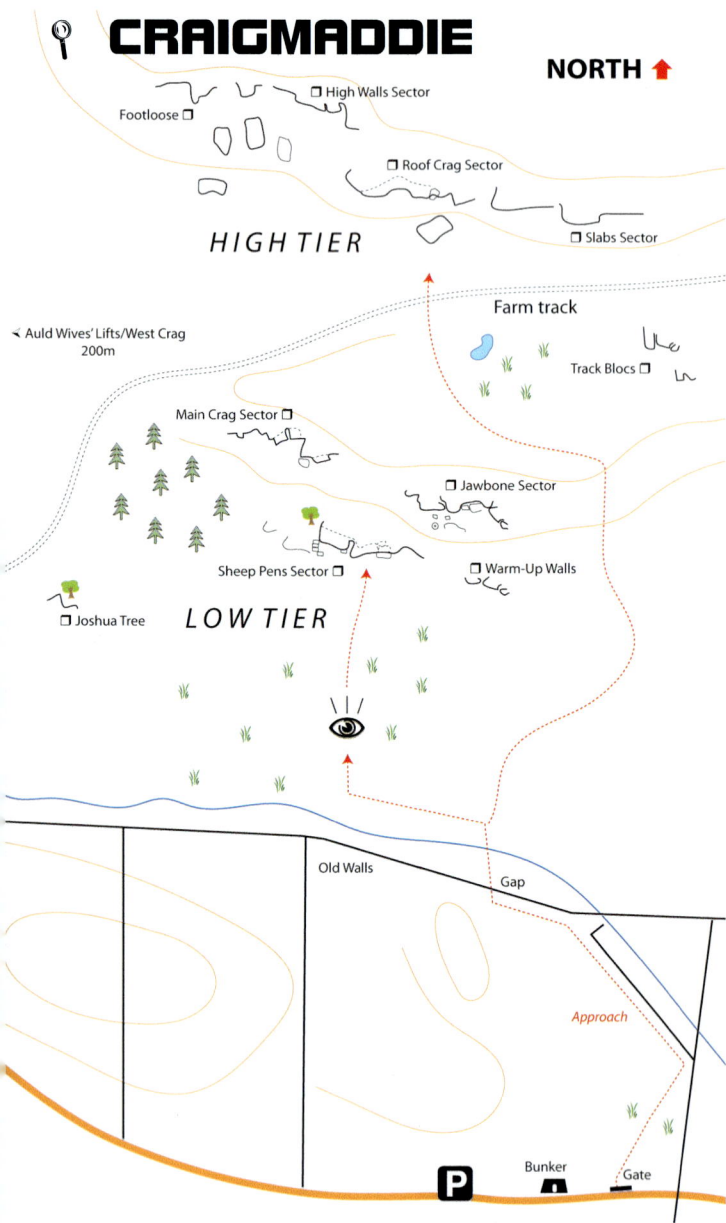

# CRAIGMADDIE

**NORTH** ↑

Footloose □
□ High Walls Sector

□ Roof Crag Sector

□ Slabs Sector

*HIGH TIER*

◁ Auld Wives' Lifts/West Crag
200m

Farm track

Track Blocs □

Main Crag Sector □

□ Jawbone Sector

Sheep Pens Sector □

□ Warm-Up Walls

□ Joshua Tree

*LOW TIER*

Old Walls

Gap

*Approach*

Bunker

Gate

P

## TRAVEL >>>

| | | |
|---|---|---|
| Town | >>> | Glasgow (North) |
| Sat Nav | >>> | G62 8LB (Bardowie area) |
| Parking | >>> | NS 58677 75817 /// trendy.actors.impose |
| Blocs | >>> | NS 58628 76321 /// copy.amused.boards |

Go north through the Glasgow suburbs of Bearsden and Milngavie on the A81. Once you climb the road north out of Milngavie, you pass Mugdock and Craigmaddie reservoir embankments on the left. After a few twists in the road, at a 3-way junction, take a right turn signposted Bardowie Linn (taking the north B-road, not the south). Continue uphill through the forest to North Blochairn farm at the top of the hill. 600m further along the road is limited parking in a layby on the right. Please park considerately to allow others room. The crags can be spied on the hills to the north.

## BLOC NOTES >>>

South-facing but exposed sandstone. The crags are sheltered from a north wind when bouldering can be in good nick in winter. The easier climbing is good in summer. Please follow THE RULES: Do not climb here after heavy rain as the rock is brittle; do not climb on a crag if there is a nesting bird; don't disturb livestock on the walk-in; take care over fences and stone walls and do not damage them; no climbing on the 'Auld Wives' Lifts' (historical carvings); and all dogs must be kept on leads!

## APPROACH >>>

15 minutes. This approach has been negotiated with the farmer to avoid disturbing livestock. Please don't go direct through livestock or damage walls From the parking, walk downhill to a farm gate on the left by an old WW2 bunker. Please close the gate after you enter the fields and negotiate the boggy section, then skirt the wall on the right till you reach the boundary wall, cross this at a gap. Once onto the moor, head left to cross a boggy section to the higher plateau and the top tier. Working down from here, westwards to the plantation, is the driest way to the lowest tier. Wellies are pretty much essential!

## SECTORS >>>

Low Tier: The ❑ **Warm-Up Walls** and ❑ **Sheep Pens Sector** are the first blocs encountered, with the ❑ **Main Crag** up and left beside the forestry plantation and the low ❑ **Jawbone Crag** on the right just above the Sheep Pens. The ❑ **Joshua Tree** is just in front of the plantation, and further west is a small crag just beside the erratic boulder pile that is the ❑ **Auld Wives' Lifts.**

High Tier: climb up to a boggy plateau and head up to the ❑ **High Walls** on the top left, the ❑ **Roof Crag** just lower right and the ❑ **Slabs** on the far right. There are other small slabs, blocs and walls between these main blocs.

CRAIGMADDIE SECTORS

MAIN CRAG

SHEEP PENS

JAWBONE

HIGH WALLS

SLABS

ROOF CRAG

TRACK BLOCS

Approach

WARM-UP WALLS

## WARM-UP WALLS

These are the small slabby walls just right of the sheep pens. They have some good low-level problems on big holds.

❒ 1. **Monkey Roof**                              4
Traverse left to right along the lip of the roof, step off on the right.
❒ 2. **Left Arête**                              2
Climb the left arête from its lowest point, using the right wall and the arête.
❒ 3. **Central Slab**                              2+
An enjoyable climb up the central ledges and slopey holds to jugs at the top.
❒ 4. **Right Slab**                              3
From a right-hand pocket, smear onto the slab and mantle up the ledges.
❒ 5. **Wee Pyramid Left**                              2+
Climb both arêtes to a jug at the apex, swing right to traverse off.
❒ 6. **Wee Pyramid Right**                              2
A short sequence of good flatties to the juggy ledge, traverse off right.

## SHEEP PEN SECTOR STAND-UPS

The main right-hand roof of the lower tier and the first encountered. The right face of the roof has an awkward stone plinth below, so pad this carefully.

❒ 1. **Ledge Problem**                              4
From the rock plinth, climb up through the good slopey shelf to the lip.
❒ 2. **Warm-Up Traverse**                              5
Traverse the lip right to left to mantle out just before the groove.
❒ 3. **The Plinth Left**                              6b
Take two poor twin holds on a slopey ledge (left of the better ledge), pull the feet onto smears and lunge to the top to mantle.

SHEEP PEN STAND-UPS

## SHEEP PEN SECTOR STAND-UPS

☐ 4. **Diving Board**                                    6b

Stand at the edge of the plinth, gain the high left crimp common to *Alchemy* and lurch to the top. Watch the landing!

☐ 5. **What Sheep?**                                    6c

The original stand-up precursor to *Abracadabra*, traversing left along the lip from the big pocket and jugs to mantle at the nose.

☐ 6. **Farmer's Trust** ★                                7a

From the midway holds on the lip (not the good crimps further left), finish direct through the annoyingly distant two-finger pocket. FA Peter Roy, 2010.

☐ 7. **The Fly**                                          6a

Take a left-hand lip pinch right of *The Nose* and jump up right to the hidden *Abracadabra* crimps, then press out the hanging groove direct.

☐ 8. **Mason's Traverse**                                6a+

Start in the right roof corner, hand traverse the shelf hard left to gain slots in left roof (as for *Filth*) and jump to jugs on the lip. Mantle out right in the corner, bridging allowed. FA John Watson, June 2013.

☐ 9. **Chockstoner /'The Nose'**                          6a

From the stone-choked chimney at the back of the crag, yard out to the arête using heel locks (or not), cut loose and climb on the left side of the nose on jugs to mantle the top.

☐ 10. **The Nose Variation**                              6b+

A variation, trending further right. From jugs in the corner, reach back to a roof hold, slap a left hand to holds, then gain a poor right-hand lip hold, with feet still on the shelf. Cut loose and clamp heels and toes under the roof, then boost for jugs up the nose and mantle out. Harder eliminates can be done. FA John Watson & Colin Lambton, 2012.

SHEEP PEN SIT STARTS

## SHEEP PEN SECTOR LOW STARTS

❐ **1. Hareline**                                                    6b
Sit start on the far right-hand lip, traverse left to *The Plinth* finishing moves.

❐ **2. Hare Extension**                                       6c
Climb *Hareline* but continue along the slopey ramp to finish up *Alchemy*.

❐ **3. The Plinth Right (Escape)**                  6a+
Sit start on the plinth on the sidepulls and rock up right on a smear to the wee ledge on the right, gain the top. Can be done cross-handed at the start.

❐ **4. The Plinth Right Hand**                        6b
Sit start on the rock plinth at a left-hand roof undercut and right-hand sidepull, then pull up to a right finger-jug and left-hand crimp and snap direct to the slopey ledge and mantle out the top. Or find your own method!

❐ **5. The Plinth Right (Cave)**                      6b+
Start in the cave and climb out rightwards to join *Plinth Right Hand*.

❐ **6. The Plinth Left Hand**                          6c+
Sit start on the plinth at a roof undercut and gain the bigger right side-pull, then the wee left crimp on the shield. A big move up and left gains a distant sloper pinch, then crimp a poor right ledge sloper and boost for the top.

❐ **7. The Plinth Left (Cave) ★**                    7a
Sit start in the cave and hand traverse out right over the prop bloc to gain the *Plinth Left Hand*.

❐ **8. Etiquette Prevails**                              7a+
The full traverse of *Abracadabra* from a sitting start as for *The Plinth*, with a crux sequence low left to gain the main traverse. FA Peter Roy, 2019.

❐ **9. Abracadabra ★**                                   7a
From a crouching start at the block under the right roof (no block on right), heel hook back to the lip, gain the large pocket and flat holds, then traverse with interest left along the lip to mantle out at the nose.

❏ 10. **Abracadabra Extension**                    7a+

*Abracadabra* but continue left round *The Nose* and reverse *Colin and John's Stellar Adventure* to step off on the left of that roof. FA Brendan Croft, 2014.

❏ 11. **Farmer's Trust (Cave)**                    7b

Start as for *Abracadabra* at the back of the cave and climb most of this problem to gain the direct of the original. FA Peter Roy.

❏ 12. **Alchemy ★**                    7c

Roof start as for *Abracadabra*, but from the pocket cross the left hand to a crimp and right to a slopey pinch, then gain a left-hand crimp above and dyno to the lip. FA Ben Litster, 2008.

❏ 12a. **Smoke and Mirrors**                    7b+

Essentially a more direct version of *Alchemy* taking the good ledge hold with the left hand and the crimp with the right, then boosting for the crimp high right, a bit morpho, then crank to the top. FA Stewart Cable, 2021.

❏ 12b. **Lockdown Alchemist**                    7b

Climb *Lockdown Lockoff* but instead of directly topping out, traverse left and finish up the end of *Alchemy*. FA David Elder, 2020.

❏ 12c. **Alchemist's Trust**                    7c

Climb *Alchemy* to match the high crimp before the lip, traverse left through the pocket of *Farmer's Trust*, right hand into a sloper sidepull, left into good sidepull, mantle out left. No lip allowed until the topout. FA David Elder, 2020.

❏ 13. **Alakazaam**                    7c

The original hard traverse from the right along the slopey ledge to drop down through *Alchemy* to finish along *Abracadabra*. A sit start on the right can be done but doesn't add to the grade. FA Mike Lee, 2012.

❏ 14. **Lockdown Lockoff**                    6c+

The overlap sit start on the right, with a right hand on a good crimp and left hand on an undercling. Lock off with the right hand and bump left into another undercling, then throw into the ledge jug, mantle out. FA Jack McCamley, 2020.

❏ 15. **Necromancy**                    7c

Sit start as for *Lockdown Lockoff*, traverse left to the *Alchemy* crimp, pull left through the pocket of *Farmer's Trust*, drop down to lip crimps of *Abracadabra* and finish up this. A finish via *Farmer's Trust* makes it 7b+. FA David Elder, 2020

❏ 16. **Esper**                    7c

Not a sit, but a low start at the back of the sheep pen roof. Reach out to the lip, then use the roof crack to climb through the lip into a finish along *Abracadabra*. FA David Elder, 2021.

❏ 17. **Farmagician**                    7c+

Start at the back of the cave with hands on the low bloc, as for *Esper*, and climb through the roof via small edges and the big roof crack to gain the lip. Finish via *Farmer's Trust* without using the good handrail out left. FA David Elder, 2021.

❏ 18. **The Magic ★**                    8a

A hard and excellent technical problem. Climb through the central roof of *Esper* and finish rightwards up *Alchemy*. Needs dry conditions for the roof section. FA David Elder, 2021.

SHEEP PEN LEFT

## SHEEP PEN LEFT
The left roof is only good when dry, usually only in summer.

☐ 1. **Filth**                                              6a
Gain a roof slot in the right-hand side of the overhang and dyno for jugs on the lip, work right to mantle out above the corner between the two roofs.

☐ 2. **Predator Roof**                                      6a+
A sit start to *Filth*. Sit start the blunt shelf-end arête and gain a jug flange on the roof, reach back and left to the jug rail, match and cross over to the jugs on the nose out right, mantle out the corner.

☐ 3. **Predator Roof Rocket**                               6b+
Start on the blunt shelf and gain the juggy crimp on the right then a smaller crimp on the left. A big move or dyno gains the nose and top out to the right in the corner. The landing may need several pads. FA Jack McCamley, June 2020.

☐ 4. **Colin and John's Stellar Adventure**                 6b
A neglected adventure along the lip of the left roof. Sit start hard left in the cave at the leaning prop block, reach back to jugs, then heel-hook and cross all the way along the lip to a rest of sorts at the double jug rail, then grab the jugs on the nose and mantle the corner, bridging allowed. FA Colin Lambton & John Watson, 2013.

☐ 5. **Short Nose**                                         4
Down left of the roof are two low prows. This climbs the right one from a sit start at the left edge of the low vegetated wall.

☐ 6. **Short Nose Righthand**                               6a
Sit start start slightly right of original with feet in a wee cave and climb directly up through slopers and crimps, not using the left arête.

☐ 7. **Overhanging Nose**                                   4
Sit start the wee prow a few metres up left, mainly on its left side.

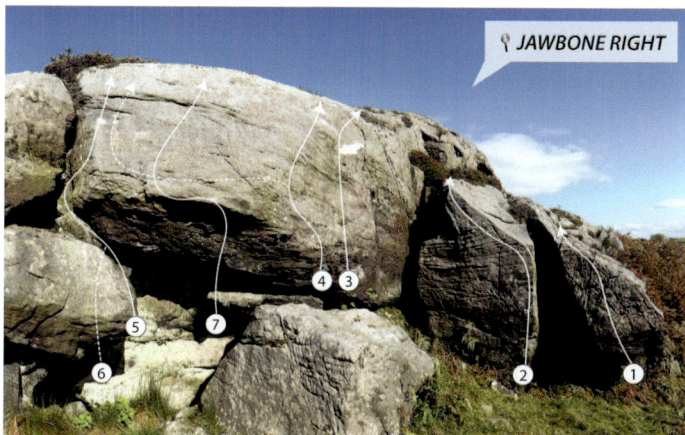

## JAWBONE CRAG RIGHT

The lipped right roof above the plinth of rock has some good problems with balancy topouts on the slab.

◻ 1. **Right Arête**                    3
Sit start the wee buttress via its blunt arête, climb to the lip and rock over onto the top.

◻ 2. **Next Arête**                    3+
Sit start the arête left of the corner, via pockets to tricky slopers on the lip, leading up left to a jug and mantle.

◻ 3. **Right Wall**                    3+
Climb the right wall off the raised plinth, trending right from good holds. Careful at the top as the holds are hidden and the landing is bad.

◻ 4. **Jawline**                    5+
Step off the left side of the plinth and climb onto the slab via slopers. May need a brush first. Variation: finish via a foot traverse along the lip of the slab.

◻ 5. **Jawbone**                    4
Gain the corner and mantle onto the slab of the hanging roof's left arête, using feet on the ramp and anything else. Pad the landing.

◻ 6. **Gnasher**                    5+
Sit start the bulge under the left of the roof, at a left-hand side-pull and right-hand pocket. Gain flat holds on the ledge and mantle up to the big corner.

◻ 7. **Hamstrung** ★                    6c+
Sit start in the cave at the big flange feature, gain good holds on the overhung lip and use a high right heel to get established on the slab above. Desperate and likely to tweak your hamstrings! FA Simon Smith, 2015.

JAWBONE LEFT

## JAWBONE CRAG LEFT

☐ 8. **Extreme John**        6c

An extension to *Cantilever*, this is the full low right-to-left hand-traverse of the undercut lip of the Jawbone crag. Sit start in the cave at a large right-facing flake, climb technically left on the lip to gain the midway niche, then do the crux of *Cantilever* and finish up jugs round the left edge of crag. FA Colin Lambton, 2012.

☐ 9. **Uni Lever**        5+

Sit start at lip crimps on the right side of the lip and gain the slopey break, then mantle up onto the higher slabs. FA John Watson & Colin Lambton, 2012.

☐ 10. **Cantilever ★**        6b

Sit start in the middle lip at niche jugs and lip traverse left with a superb horizontal cantilever move to eventually gain the *Far Left Arête*. FA Colin Lambton & John Watson, 2012.

☐ 11. **Short Lever**        4+

Sit start as for *Cantilever* but go straight up.

☐ 12. **Cannae Lever**        6a

A sloper problem. Sit start the arête left of *Cantilever* and traverse right on lip slopers. Bridge to the start niche of *Cantilever* and use a wall sloper to gain the break. Mantle up to slabs. FA John Watson, 2019.

☐ 13. **Far Left Arête**        3+

Stand start the short left arête and climb up through a break onto scrittly slabs to finish out left.

☐ 14. **Diversion**        6a

Up and left of the Jawbone crag (left of a chasm) is a very short wall with a groove. Sit start this and onto the slab.

MAIN CRAG

## MAIN CRAG SECTOR

☐ 1. **Fuel-Injected Shrimp**                    5

Starting at the right end of the slabby wall on the left of the crag, climb the blunt arête to gain the good horizontal ledge. Make an entertaining move to reach and then surmount the projecting prow direct. Airy.

☐ 2. **Rocket Shrimp**                    6b+

From the good incut under the arête of *Fuel-Injected*, dyno direct to the ledge.

☐ 3. **West Wall**                    6a

The west-facing wall left of the roofed grooves. Sit start and gain a left sidepull and lunge up and right to a corner hold, find a crimp for the left hand and race up through the jugs above.

☐ 4. **Roof Arête**                    6b

Sit start under the left-hand roof at the break, gain slopers on the wee hanging corner, then a hard pull on the hanging right arête allows the feet to be brought up to the lip. Finish left across the easy groove and up *West Wall*.

☐ 5. **Roof Arête Extension**                    6c

Start in a corner at the right end of the roof. Traverse the roof lip leftwards, no back wall, to finish up *Roof Arête*. FA Colin Lambton, 2012.

☐ 6. **Si's Arête**                    7a

The vague arête just left of *Roof Arête*. Sit start on jugs at the back of the roof, gain slopers on the lip and use these to gain an edge in the corner. Slap up the arête to gain better holds and a standing position. FA Simon Smith, 2012.

☐ 7. **Owl Traverse**                    6b

An extension under *Roof Arête*. Sit start far right and traverse the lip of the roof (no use of back wall) to stay low and finish up *West Wall*.

☐ 8. **Flight Path**                    6b

An overhang start from back of the troughed recess leads to awkward and strenuous moves through the bulge via the cleft. The top may need cleaned.

DOBBO'S ROOF

## DOBBO'S ROOF

Just to the right of the main crag past a low wall and around the corner is a deep low roof. The next problems tackle this.

□ 1. **The Curse of Dobbo**                    6b

A right to left traverse of the lip of the low hanging roof/slab. Sit start at jugs under the right side of the cave and gain the lip, traverse left on pockets and slopers to finish matched on the arête, step off. FA Colin Lambton & John Watson, 2012.

□ 2. **Dobbo's Roof**                    6c+

Reverse the lip of *Curse of Dobbo* left to right, then gain a good right hand side-pull and make a desperate mantle onto the slab above. Can also be climbed direct, but usually with wet roof holds. FA Brendan Croft, 2016.

□ 3. **Chossy Squeeze**                    5

Over to the left-hand side, lay back start to a nice jug, then climb through the mossy chimney. FA Matthew Deans, 2020.

## ROOF CRAG SECTOR

Most problems finish with a drop-off from high jugs, as the top is vegetated, but some gardening may make top-outs more amenable.

□ 1. **BA**                    6a+

Sit start jugs on the roof on its lower left side and pull through on sloping crimps to rock over left to a big pocket and easy finish up the slab.

❑ 2. **Short Haul**                              6b
Sit start at starting holds of *BA*, bum-scrape left to finish on ledges. Awkward.

❑ 3. **Long Haul**                              7a
A left-to-right traverse of the roof. Start at *BA* and traverse along the lip (no big pocket) to join the horizontal crack of *Buzz*. Drop down to the jugs on *Oxygen Mask* then go right to finish up jugs on right arête. FA Brendan Croft, 2014.

❑ 4. **Easyjet**                              6c+
Sit start very low in the cave on flat holds under the far left of the roof, throw in a heel hook and gain a left-hand pinch under the lip, then slap right along the lip crimps to join *Buzz* and rock over. Not easy at all, ruined two pairs of 5.10s on first ascent. FA John Watson & Colin Lambton, 2006.

❑ 5. **Easyjet Direct** ★                    7a
Sit start as for *Easyjet* but go direct over the roof on lip crimps to the big pocket and finish up the slab. Often considered a better and harder finish to the original 'escape' right. FA Colin Lambton, 2012.

❑ 6. **Buzz**                              6c
Lie-down start at the low central slots of the cave, place a heel high right, then pull on to a layaway and boost up left to the horizontal crack, then mantle onto the slabs.

❑ 7. **Ici Kirkintilloch**                      6c
Start as for Buzz but follow the horizontal crack left to finish up *Easyjet Direct*.

❑ 8. **Last Call for Passenger Coll**          7a+
Start up *Buzz* then traverse left along the horizontal crack and pockets to a crux drop-down to gain the starting holds of *BA*. The original finished along *Short Haul* at the same grade but is awkward. FA Colin Lambton, 2013.

❑ 9. **Project**                              P
Sit start the low jugs of the roof and climb the roof direct to a mantle.

**ROOF CRAG CENTRAL**

1
2
3
4

**ROOF CRAG RIGHT**

4
5
6
7
8
9

Forgotten Arête

❐ 10. **Oxygen Mask** 6b

Sit start the low jugs of the roof and boost up right to tan-coloured sloper crimps, then crank to the sharp jugs. Mantle out or drop off.

❐ 11. **Cryanair** 6b

Sit start from good holds under the right arête by the separated plinth, break left through the slopers to lunge for lip jugs. Drop off.

❐ 12. **Bam or Boulderer?** 5+

Sit start jugs and climb the arête to a tricky mantle. *Boulderer or Bam* is a variation into the crack via a finger-lock (5+). FA Stuart Burns, 2018.

## ROOF CRAG CENTRAL

❐ 1. **The Snap** 6c

Sit start on the detached plinth, both hands matching lip crimp. Boost left to holds on the left of the crack, then gain a crack slot and pocket to a mantle.

❐ 2. **Panoramix** 7a+

Mantle left onto the hanging slab via a shallow pocket, the crux just getting your feet off the ground. Traverse off left. FA Jack McKechnie, 2021.

❐ 3. **Project** P

A longstanding project climbing the crack and scooped wall. Use crimp sidepulls in the crack and out right to pull on and gain the top. A sit start may be a very high grade.

## ROOF CRAG RIGHT

❐ 4. **Emirates Wall** 5

Get stood on the wall via a gaston and high right crimp, then traverse right along crimps to the big hole and then the corner.

❐ 5. **The Corner** 3

Layback the ramped corner to gain jugs up right, mantle onto the slab and descend this. A cramped bridging sit start is Font 5.

❐ 6. **Plinth Eliminate** 6b

Sit start left of the arête via crimps only, crossing to a high central crimp (crux) to chicken-heads to gain jugs at top. FA John Watson, 2015.

❐ 7. **Plinth Arête** 5+

Sit start on a low separated plinth on its far right and slap up to jugs on the arête and rock out right at the top, downclimb *Easy Slab* for descent.

❐ 8. **Plinthless Arête** 6a

Sit start *Plinth Arête* pulling on with heels from sitting, no feet on the plinth.

❐ 9. **Easy Slab** 2

The slab right of *Plinth Arête* to a scramble right to descend (or downclimb).

❐ 10. **Forgotten Arête** 5+

The nice arête between the main roof crag area and the *Pale Slab* area. Sit start the arête to a jug of glory on the lip, then rock over right onto the slab.

THE SLABS

## THE SLABS SECTOR

These are the pale slabs on the far right of the high tier (not the scrappy higher ones to the left). They are still quite highball and need care.

☐ 1. **The Pale Slab** ★                    4+

Highball. From the left ledge, pull onto the wall and step right delicately onto the slab, wobble up this directly on polished crimps.

☐ 2. **Right Slab**                    4

From the undercut cave corner, pull onto the slab with an awkward move to an easier crack. Tiptoe to the top.

☐ 3. **Hilary Mantle**                    6b+

The roof to the right of *Right Slab*. Gain holds on the lip and rock over or, more usually, belly-flop onto the slab using a left sidepull.

☐ 4. **Hilary Wall**                    4

The wall right of *Hilary Mantle* climbed via an undercut. Highball finish straight up the slab.

## TRACK BLOCS

These short walls sit down and east of the slabs area below the track. They are a little lichenous but good fun.

❑ 1. **Track Traverse**                    3+

Pull on at the bottom of the left wall and traverse the lip up and left to a rockover finish above a large pocket.

❑ 2. **Easy Route/Descent**                    1+

Pull onto the rib's ramp and climb to the top in easy steps. Can also be used as a descent.

❑ 3. **Left Edge**                    3+

Stand start. Use holds in the stone-choked crack to aid a pull over the left lip onto the top.

❑ 4. **Track Wall**                    5+

Sit start. Pull up to twin crimps then lunge up and right to lip holds, mantle over the top to finish.

❑ 5. **Pocket Problem**                    4

Sit start the right edge via a large pocket to jugs and a mantle out left.

❑ 6. **Flake Pinnacle**                    2

A nice little slabby pinnacle wall facing south, 10m below the problems described above. Use good holds to climb the wall centrally to jugs.

HIGH WALLS

★ *Si Smith on Undercutter Crack*

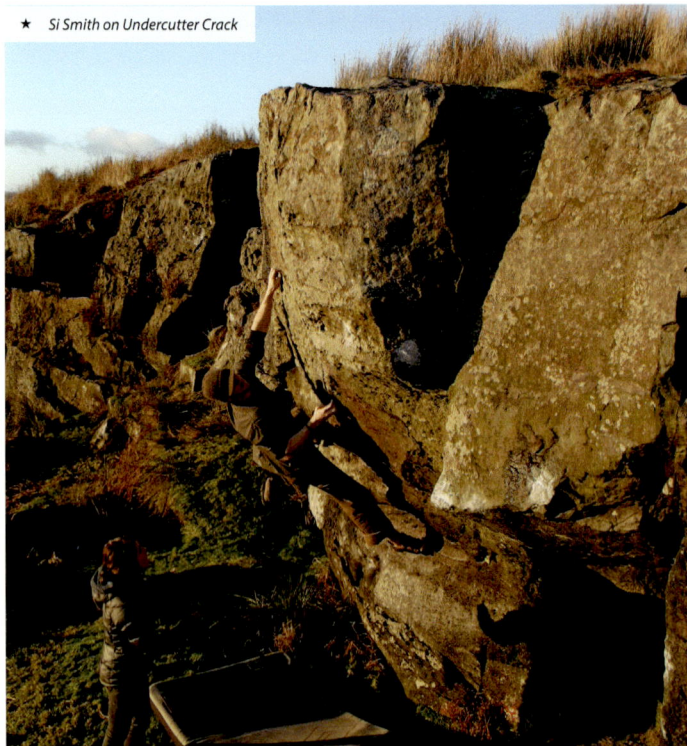

## HIGH WALLS

Excellent flat landings make this a popular wall. Many link-ups can be done.

❑ 1. **Left Mantle**                                      6b

The far left of the sloping ramp with a wee corner at the top and jug on lip.

❑ 2. **The Mantle**                                       6b

Gain the sloping ramp centrally, without recourse to the corners, mantle out directly. Infuriatingly good fun.

❑ 3. **Pocket Eliminate**                                 5

Sit start at a deep pocket and crimp. Climb up to the wee hanging corner to the right of *The Mantle* without using any holds in *Left Crack*.

❑ 4. **Left Crack**                                       4

The crack just right of the sloping ramp shelf's wee corner, with a long reach.

❑ 5. **Right Crack**                                      5

A little harder. Pull on at the jugs and gain a right sidepull on the wall. Use this to step up onto the jugs and gain the top.

❑ 6. **Flake Wall**                                       6a+

The wall just right of the cracks. Start at jugs and gain the flake to twist up to a very sharp left-hand crimp, then go for the top. Sit start is the same grade.

❑ 7. **Undercutter Crack** ★                              6a+

Use the flared crack to undercut up to crimps on the wall, then climb direct to the top. Various link-ups can be done.

❑ 7a. **Magnum Classic**                                  7a+

Start as for *Flake Wall Sit* on jugs then traverse right and up the prow without using anything right of the large crack. FA David Elder, 2020

❑ 8. **Right Arête**                                      6a+

Using the flared crack and the big crack on the right, rock up right around the bulging arête onto the nose jugs, then finish up the blunt arête above.

❑ 9. **Right Crack Direct**                               6b+

From the base of the crack gain a sidepull halfway up the crack and rock over onto the nose. Use a small edge near the top of the crack to aid the topout.

❑ 10. **Twister** ★                                       6b+

Sit start the right roof and gain the lip then the jug on the lip. Cross over left to a hidden crimp pocket on the bulge and finish direct up the wall and arête.

❑ 10a. **Twister Traverse**                               7a

A harder finish left along the wall on crimps to *Left Crack*. FA John Craven, 2021.

❑ 11. **King-O-The-Bongo**                                6b+

Sit start the roof to a pinch then over the lip to a sloper/crimp, use a gaston to gain the crack. Does not use the far right arête.

❑ 12. **Twister Direct**                                  7b

Eliminate. Sit start and gain the lip, then pull on slopers to a direct rock-over onto the slab. No left crack or right arête. 7a+ stand. FA Lewis Roy, 2019.

❑ 13. **Far Right Problem**                               5

The far right arête of the flying lip, left arête allowed at start.

❑ 14. **High Crag Traverse**                              6b

Traverse the wall low from the far left to finish up *Far Right Problem*.

FOOTLOOSE

MINI-RIDER

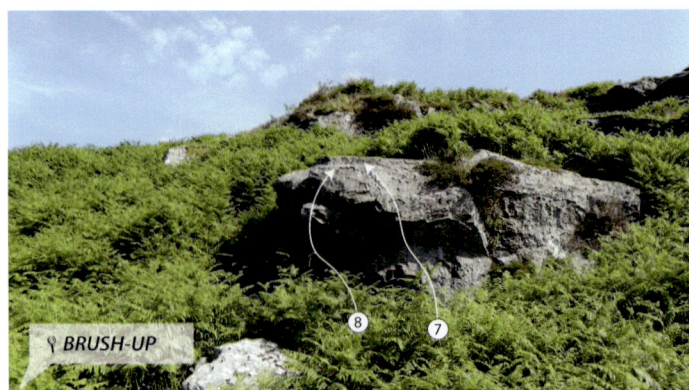

BRUSH-UP

About 15m to the left of High Walls are various low blocs with good traverses and some sit start straight-ups. They tend to disappear behind the bracken in summer and are best in winter, spring and late autumn.

❑ 1. **The Roof**                                5

Just left of *The Mantle* on the High Walls sector is a hanging roof. Monkey left then back right.

❑ 2. **Footloose**                                6b

This is a long low outcrop with a surprisingly good low hand traverse. Sit start just right of the nose and traverse leftwards round the nose to the corner. Continue low left on slopey top ledges to a short mantle at the very end of the buttress.

❑ 3. **Drag and Drop**                                5+

Mantle in the middle of *Footloose*. Sit start at two good holds in the crack right of the corner, gain the left lip, then mantle the large flat ledge.

❑ 4. **Mini-Rider**                                5

Just below and east of *Footloose* is a low flying lip. Traverse the lip from a right spike to the far left and mantle. No back or feet on the prop bloc.

❑ 5. **Mini-Rider Extension**                                6b

Sit start at a separated ledge on the right on slopers and make a crux dyno or heel-mantle up to the spike jug on the lip to finish left along *Mini-Rider*. FA John Watson, 2017.

❑ 6. **Stick to the Lip**                                6a

Eliminate but good. Traverse the easy lip up and left to use only a moon-shaped dish to match slopers and gain the left edge. Can also be climbed as a straight-up mantle through the sloper at about the same grade.

❑ 7. **Brush Up Central**                                4

The wee wall bloc just west of and below *Mini-Rider*. Sit start in the centre and climb over onto the flat top.

❑ 8. **Brush Up Left**                                3

The wee wall bloc just west of and below *Mini-Rider*. Sit start the left arête and climb over via jugs onto the flat top.

★ *John Watson on Joshua Tree*

## JOSHUA TREE

This is the wee crag by the ancient rowan tree, beside the track, in front of the spruce plantation. It's on the way to the *Auld Wives' Lifts*.

❏ 1. **Joshua Tree**                                    5+

Sit start under the roof and bridge up via an undercut to gain pockets and ledges. Climb through the top with a fun cross-over crux to the apex. A sit start to the left is maybe a little harder, not using the foot ramp on the right.

## WEST CRAG

This is the slabby east-facing wall to the west of the *Auld Wives' Lifts* erratics. Note: there is no climbing allowed on the *Auld Wives' Lifts* erratic boulder due to ancient carvings.

❏ 1. **Right Slab**                                    2

The right-hand slab with carved names: *P. Pyne 1977 Philomena*.

❏ 2. **The Rib**                                    4

Sit start the flaked right rib of slab, gain a standing position via the pocket and finish direct.

❏ 3. **Druid's Problem**                                    6a

Sit start as for *The Groove*, but traverse right to the central lip and mantle onto the slab. Tricky and good.

❏ 4. **The Groove**                                    4+

Sit start the groove and mantle into it, finish up and right.

❏ 5. **The Magic Eye**                                    2

Step onto the slab on the corner and trend left. Check the 'Egyptian Eye' carving 30m to the left.

WEST CRAG

# □ LENNOXTOWN

LOVER'S LEAP ROOF

LOVER'S LEAP CRAG

## BLOC NOTES >>>

Effectively the 'dark side' of Craigmaddie Muir, the dispersed rock outcrops and boulders on this northerly escarpment are greener and require a good dry spell. The rock is part of the same basal sandstone outcropping around Craigmaddie Muir. The rock is compact in parts but can have brittle holds. The highlight is the Lover's Leap roof and the Dark Side bloc further west.

## TRAVEL >>>

| Town | >>> | Lennoxtown |
|---|---|---|
| Sat Nav | >>> | G66 7BB |
| Parking | >>> | NS 61486 78575 ///vote.rooms.viewer |
| Lover's Leap | >>> | NS 60252 78254 ///data.adjuster.panel |
| The Dark Side | >>> | NS 59230 78103 ///variously.important.foil |

Lennoxtown is a small town at the foot of the Campsie hills 10 miles north of Glasgow. From Lennoxtown, follow the A891 'Glen Road' north-west past a roundabout for 1km. The next wee roundabout turns left into Campsie Village housing estate. Park in a small layby just across the river on the right. Follow the track west to drop down to a bridge by the river after 200m. Continue along the track south of the river to a widening tarmac road winding up to the ruins of Woodhead House. Walk right around the ruins to a track leading into the woods west along the top of an escarpment. Five minutes' walk leads to the old metal railing viewpoint of ❏ **Lover's Leap**. Just before this is a steep slope leading down to the hidden roof just east of the crag. For ❏ **The Dark Side** continue from Lover's Leap west for 1km along the escarpment, keeping to the main track which swings south. Towards the end of the forestry section, cut back north to the forest edge and head west again. Look out for a small burn running down towards Craigend Farm. Follow this downhill to the field boundary where you might find the blocs.

## LOVER'S LEAP PROBLEMS >>>

❏ 1. **Gordon Bombay** ★      *Lover's Leap*      7b+
Climb out of the roof to the lip jugs. Continue backwards under the roof using heels and compression moves to finish up the left arête. FA Alex Gorham, 2013.

❏ 2. **Ben Quest**      *Lover's Leap*      6a
From under the roof, reach back to the lip and traverse left to finish up via a flake on the wall.

❏ 3. **Chickenhead**      *Lover's Leap*      5+
Climb the short wall via pockets and edges into the dirty groove.

❏ 4. **The Clamp**      *Lover's Leap*      6b
Sit start the right arête and trend left up the higher wall.

❏ 5. **Wow Jen** ★      *Lover's Leap*      6c
Sit start the pillar on the right of the roof.

❏ 6. **Magic Carpet Ride**      *Lover's Leap*      7a
Stand start to the wall and arête bloc below the roof.

★ *Thom Davies on Solus Rex*

★ *Short Wall*

## THE DARK SIDE PROBLEMS >>>

☐ 1. **Solus Rex** ★           *Dark Side*          7c+
*The Dark Side* direct without using the foot-ramp, smearing onto the edge of the roof instead, cross over to a pinch, gain a high left hold and top out direct. FA Thom Davies, October 2020.

☐ 2. **The Dark Side** ★         *Dark Side*          7a
Sit start jugs at the back right of the cave up to a large hole on the lip. Cross and twist off a foot-ramp on the right to gain sidepulls on the face, then top-out left and centrally. FA John Watson, 2013.

☐ 3. **Short Wall**            *Dark Side*          4
Sit start the wall 10m metres to the right and mantle.

*DARK SIDE BLOC*

# □ CAMPSIE BLOCS

WEST BLOCS

CROW ROAD

EAST BLOCS

Parking

CAMPSIE BLOCS

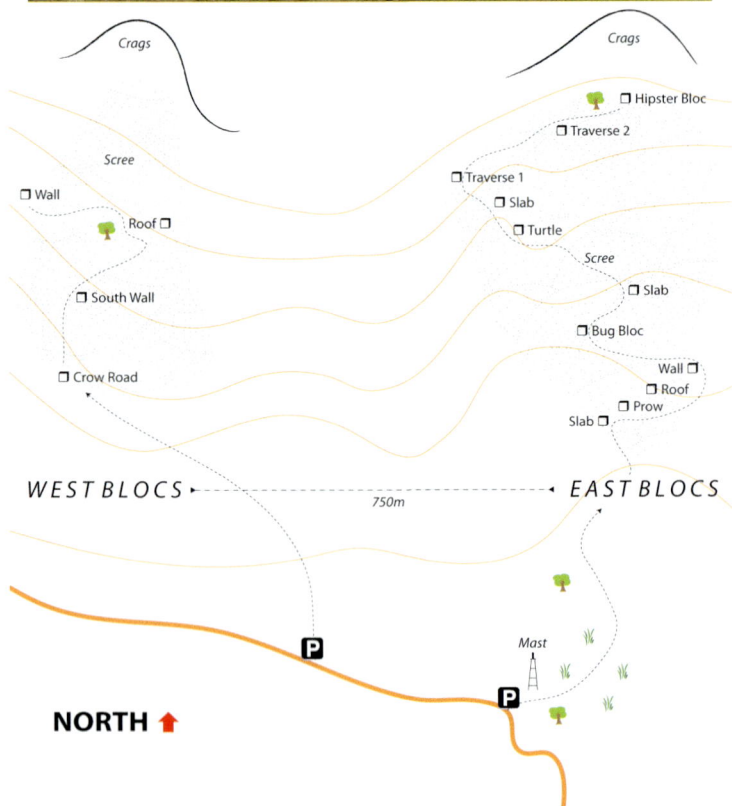

Crags

Crags

□ Hipster Bloc

□ Traverse 2

Scree

□ Traverse 1

□ Wall

□ Slab

Roof □

□ Turtle

Scree

□ South Wall

□ Slab

□ Bug Bloc

□ Crow Road

Wall □

□ Roof

□ Prow

Slab □

*WEST BLOCS*

750m

*EAST BLOCS*

**NORTH** ⬆

Mast

P

P

### BLOC NOTES >>>

'The Crow Road' rises out of Lennoxtown in steep switchbacks beloved of cyclists under the Campsie Fells. North of the road, on the flanks of the escarpment of Cort-ma Law, scree slips and small boulders litter the slopes. There are two main sectors of bouldering: one on the west and another to the east above the communications mast by the golf course. Though nowhere at all big, there are plenty of short problems and traverses for a good low-grade circuit, great for kids or older climbers worried about their hips. Watch out for friable rock, and bring a good brush for cleaning. Best in spring and autumn. .

### TRAVEL >>>

| Town | >>> | Lennoxtown |
|------|-----|-----------|
| Sat Nav | >>> | G66 7NU |
| Parking | >>> | NS 62351 79262 ///marriage.fallback.silently |
| West Blocs | >>> | NS 62142 79596 ///lecturing.contracts.friend |
| East Blocs | >>> | NS 62859 79183 ///like.supported.girder |

Head north out of Glasgow to Lennoxtown, just under the Campsie Fells on the A891. This can also be gained from Strathblane and the A81 from the west. Follow the 'Crow Road' north out of the town from the shops junction, which winds up past the golf course. After the steep swithcbacks, park a few hundred metres uphill in a layby on the right. For the ❑ **East Sector** under 'Sloughmuclock' (it means 'hollow of the clocks' in Gaelic), contour towards the mast and up to the scree. For the ❑ **West Sector,** under 'Black Craig', stomp leftwards up the hill until the hidden boulders come into view on a grassy alp.

### WEST SECTOR >>>

❑ 1. **The Crow Road** ★                                    6b+

Sit start the prow and gain slopers on the lip, then crank right to a sharp hold and continue to a good orange hold on the lip, rock over onto the slab to finish.

❑ 2. **The Crow's Mantle**                                   5+

The last part of the sit start, this circuit problem mantles onto the slab from good holds.

❑ 3. **Pete's Arête**                                        5

Crow Road boulder. Climb the arête on the slabby left side, good technical fun.

❑ 4. **Colin's Roof**                                        6c+

The orange cave at the back of the Crow Road boulder can be climbed from a low sit start to an awkward pull over onto the wall.

❑ 5. **South Wall**                                          6b

A wall and bulge on a south-facing boulder at the base of the scree.

❑ 6. **South Wall Traverse**                                 5

A right-to-left traverse of the same boulder.

❑ 7. **East Wall**                                           4

A wall facing east at the left side of the scree field.

❑ 8. **Roof**                                                6a

A right-to-left traverse and mantle of the roof on the east side of the scree.

CAMPSIES EAST

TRAVERSE 2
TRAVERSE 1
TURTLE
SLAB 2
LOW WALL
STINK BUG
SLAB 1
ROOF
PROW

★ The Crow Road

❑ 9. **Groove Slab**                                                    2
Easy warm-up cracked groove at the bottom of the slope.

❑ 10. **Prow Bloc**                                                     3+
Mantle the short wall left of the low prow at the base of the slope.

❑ 11. **Roof Bloc**                                                     4+
Sit start the square-cut roof climbing up its left side.

❑ 12. **Masters Wall**                                                  5
A low wall overlooking the gold course. Sit start the right wall and arête .

❑ 13. **Masters Cave**                                                  4+
Sit start the niche or cave on the left side of the wall.

❑ 14. **The Bug**                                                       6a
A low roof about halfway up the hill. Mantle onto the left slab with a heel.

❑ 14a. **Stink Bug**                                                    7a
Traverse the roof from a far left sit start to mantle into the stand-up.

❑ 15. **Slab**                                                          3
Climb the central slab groove on small holds initially.

❑ 16. **The Turtle**                                                    5
Sit on wee bloc and traverse left on the lip under the left head of 'the turtle'.

❑ 17. **Slab**                                                          3+
Short undercut slab to its apex from good holds. Faces south down wee valley.

❑ 18. **Traverse 1**                                                    5
Crouch start roof bloc on left at a slot and lip traverse right to turn the edge.

❑ 19. **Traverse 2**                                                    4
Very low long bloc at the top. Traverse from left jugs to a far right mantle.

❑ 20. **Hipster Prow**                                                  5+
Mantle the wee prow right of a hawthorn tree at the edge of the corrie. A sit start is 6b.

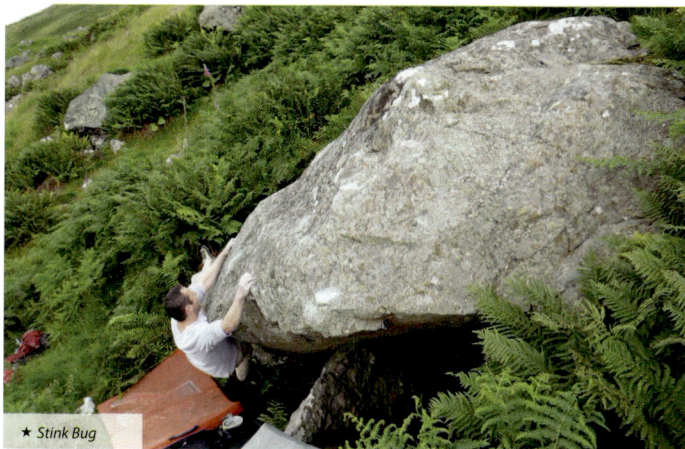

★ *Stink Bug*

# ❏ CROY HILL

### NORTH ↑
1KM

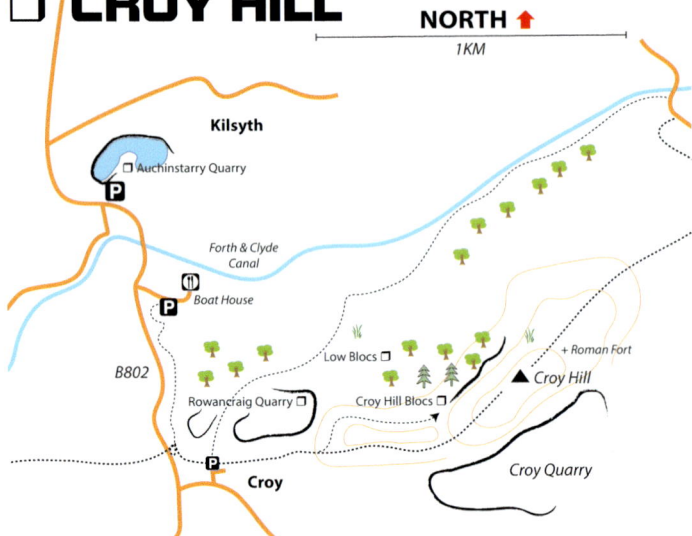

Kilsyth

❏ Auchinstarry Quarry

🅿

Forth & Clyde Canal

🅿 Boat House

Low Blocs ❏

+ Roman Fort

B802

▲ Croy Hill

Rowancraig Quarry ❏

Croy Hill Blocs ❏

🅿

Croy

Croy Quarry

## BLOC NOTES >>>

Bouldering for the Romans! Situated north-east of Glasgow in the Kelvin valley around Croy Hill and Kilsyth, bouldering can be found along the Antonine Wall on associated basalt quarries and blocs. The famous trad quarry that is Auchinastarry has a few problems and a good east-facing boulder wall, and other quarries and blocs in the area have potential for further exploration.

## TRAVEL >>>

| | | |
|---|---|---|
| Town | >>> | Croy |
| Sat Nav | >>> | G65 9JF |
| Croy Hill Parking | >>> | NS 72270 76203 /// unimpeded.boils.blitz |
| Croy Hill | >>> | NS 73003 76392 /// sorters.life.smuggled |

Set your Sat Nav off the M80 for roundabout world! Or get the train to Croy. Access for Croy Hill can be made from limited parking spaces at the very west end of Croy before it hits the main road. Join the Antonine Wall path heading due east uphill to Croy Hill. After going through a metal gate onto the hillside, turn off left into a small subsidiary valley on the north escarpment of Croy Hill (the rock here is poor). Follow a rough trail east through the valley to a wooded area. A north-facing series of blocs and pinnacles continues east under the trees. They provide some good problems on slopey dolerite, though they often require good cleaning. Beware the sloping landings, bring tent pegs to pin down your mat, and be careful with brittle rock, especially on highballs.

☐ KILOWATT BLOC

☐ WEE ROOF

☐ WHALE BLOC

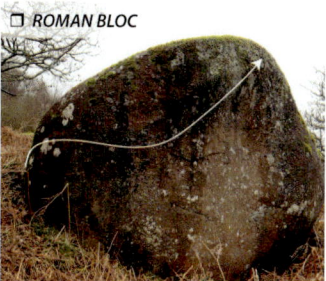
☐ ROMAN BLOC

## TOP PROBLEMS >>>

☐ 1. **Kilowatt Prow**                    5+
A bloc at the west end of the crag.
Step off the right ledge to climb the
prow to a hollow flake mantle.

☐ 2. **Kilowatt ★**                          6c
The wall from an undercut direct over
a gaston and poor slopers.

☐ 3. **Kilowatt Right**                    6a
A variation crossing the left hand all
the way to the far right hold.

☐ 4. **Wee Roof Slab**                     5
A short roof and slab with a beech on
top, about 15m further along. From
the double crimp mantle onto the
slab.

☐ 5. **Wee Roof Sit**                       6a
From the poor sloper at the base,
gain the good double crimp and
mantle up onto the slab.

☐ 6. **Wee Roof Slab**                    3+
From a stand start on small sidepulls
on the right, mantle left onto the
slopey ledge and finish easily.

☐ 7. **The Ledge Bloc**                   4+
A small pillar at the very top of the
slope further along. From the left
gain the pyramidal hold and mantle
the ledge to the rounded top.

A highball series of pinnacles
follows which may be top-roped. The
boulders then reduce in height
towards the east end.

☐ 8. **Whale Bloc**                           5
Marking the east end is a low slab
bloc with a quarrier's drill hole. It
looks a bit like a whale. Use the old
drill hole to mantle onto the narrow
slab and climb this to the top.

☐ 9. **Roman Bloc**                           P
A project bloc at the base of the
woods nearer the quarry path.

# ☐ AUCHINSTARRY

CARPARK SECTOR

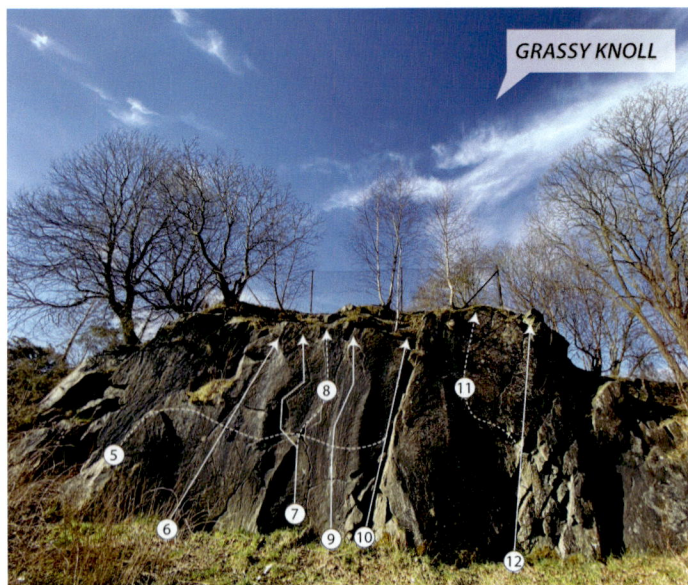

GRASSY KNOLL

## TRAVEL >>>

| Town | >>> | Kilsyth |
| Sat Nav | >>> | G65 0TD |
| Auchinstarry | >>> | NS 71950 77062 /// fells.declares.aquatics |

There is ample free parking at Auchinstarry loch in front of the big main crag.

## TOP PROBLEMS >>>

### ❏ Carpark Area

On the left of the carpark under the trees and left of the main routes, is a wall of bouldering height. It is now largely overgrown with ivy, but some gardening might reveal the old problems, though the council's landscaping may have affected the height of the problems. The best of the old problems are:

❏ 1. **Crimpy Wall**  6a
The wall right of the flake via small holds, mantle the top on slopers.

❏ 2. **Thin Crack**  5
The thin crack, grabbing the tree at the top.

❏ 3. **Bruddaz Gonna Work it Out**  6c
A left-to-right low traverse to the big groove on the right (the route *Green Onions*).

Along the crag on the right of the big *Nijinski* arête and at the end of the right wall is a highball pinnacle next to the loch.

❏ 4. **Plumline Crack**  5+
The thin but still highball,crack on the pillar. Descend the back by a  scramble.

### ❏ Grassy Knoll

This 5m wall sits on the east side of a landscaped mound beside the centre of the loch.  The thin seam crack on the right wall has yet to be climbed.

❏ 5. **Jerk Out**  6a
Stand start at the far left end under a tree, both hands on a nose of rock. Traverse left to right and reach across a blank wall into the crack, finish up this.

❏ 6. **Diagonal Crack**  3
Climb the right-trending crack just right of the left ledges.

❏ 7. **Zig Zag Crack**  3
Climb the twisty thin cracks left of the high hanging corner/arête feature.

❏ 8. **Tiny Arête**  3
Climb the wee high arête without using Zig Zag Crack for hands.

❏ 9. **Spiderman**  4
Climb the narrow wall left of the central crack via a small square crimp on the left, using the right side of *Tiny Arête* and presses on the wall.

❏ 10. **Wide Crack**  3
Climb the wide central crack on generous holds.

❏ 11. **Boulder Wall ★**  6b
From the crack on the right, reach left to a thin crack and crank to the top.

❏ 12. **Finger Flakes**  3
A pleasant series of broken flakes at the right end of the wall.

# CRAIG MINNAN

CRAIG MINNAN

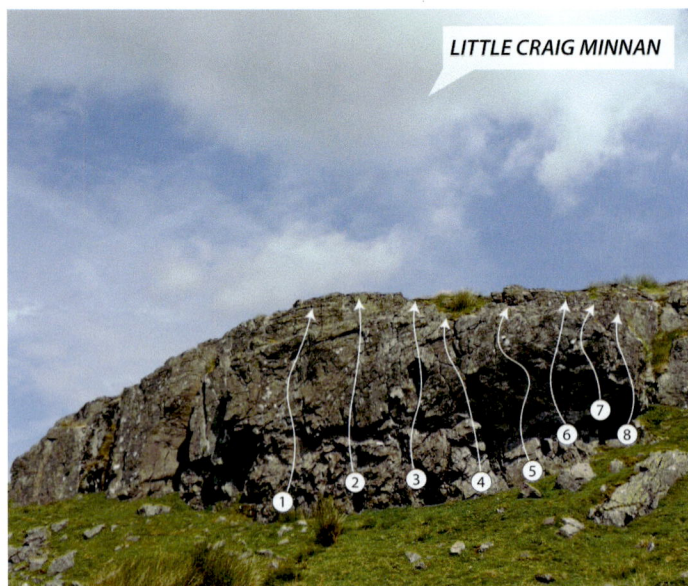

LITTLE CRAIG MINNAN

## BLOC NOTES >>>

| | | |
|---|---|---|
| Town | >>> | Lochwinnoch |
| Sat Nav | >>> | PA12 4LB |
| Parking | >>> | NS 31153 63215 /// powder.detect.unheated |
| Craig Minnan | >>> | NS 32158 64034 /// buzzards.prompts.standard |

From Lochwinnoch off the A737, follow signs north for Muirshiel Country Park to a B-road turn-off on the B786, leading in 6km to free parking at the visitor centre. Follow the red path north through woods to a path across the moor to 'Windy Hill' (1 km) and continue down and up to the crags of ◻ **Craig Minnan**. It is a boggy 10 minutes further west to ◻ **Little Craig Minnan**.

## TOP PROBLEMS CRAIG MINNAN >>>

◻ 1. **Left Arête**                                       5
The roofed arête on the left.
◻ 2. **Left Roof**                                        6a
The cracked roof on the left, from the prop pillar's break, reach back and crank!
◻ 3. **Roof Traverse**                                    5
L-R traverse under the roof to the right-hand groove to finish.
◻ 4. **Right Roof**                                       6b
Take the right roof through hard press moves.
◻ 5. **Left Wall**                                        5
The left wall direct, or from a flake on the right.
◻ 6. **Central Wall**                                     5+
The cracked central wall on the far right of the crag. Highball!
◻ 7. **Right Wall**                                       5
The right wall to a ledge, then left to a crack system. Highball!

## TOP PROBLEMS LITTLE CRAIG MINNAN >>>

◻ 1. **Cracked Groove**                                   6a
Good hanging groove snaking up the wall via a pocket.
◻ 2. **Cracked Wall**                                     6a
Gain the higher cracked wall above an overlap. A bit blind.
◻ 3. **Coffin Pod**                                       5+
Climb into the pod and escape up and left.
◻ 4. **Blaeberry Crack**                                  5
Climb the juggy crack on the left side of the barrel roof.
◻ 5. **Snake!** ★                                         6b
Climb the steep roof to a central hold, gain the snaking crack to the left to gain the top.
◻ 6. **Barrel Roof**                                      6b+
Up the central roof trending right. Steep and powerful.
◻ 7. **The Nose Left**                                    6a
Snort your way up the left side of the roof's nose on jugs to the top.
◻ 8. **The Nose Right**                                   6b
Sit start a flat hold to a press move to gain the nose. Trend right to the lip.

# □ CLOCHODRICK STONE

CLOCHODRICK SOUTH & EAST

CLOCHODRICK NORTH

## BLOC NOTES >>>

This small basalt erratic lies in the corner of a field on the outskirts of Howwood. The boulder is only three metres high at most but has some good problems and a few traverses. It is a fine spot for a summer evening. Many more eliminates and traverses can be created on this modest stone, giving it a lot more enjoyment than might be thought on first acquaintance.

## TRAVEL >>>

| Town | >>> | Howwood |
|---|---|---|
| Sat Nav | >>> | PA10 2JJ |
| Parking | >>> | NS 37344 61263 /// stretcher.goodbyes.saddens |
| Bloc | >>> | NS 37363 61275 /// ringside.thinker.doing |

From the M8 westbound after the airport, take the A737 signposted to Irvine and after about 6km take a left turn signposted Howwood. The road doubles back to the village. Take a left at the village and head over the railway bridge by the station. Continue over the Black Cart Water bridge and along the country road for two kilometres, counting to the third road on the right. Head up this for a little until the stone comes into view on the right at a junction. Park carefully in a layby and cross the electric fence at a stone stile to boulder at will.

## TOP PROBLEMS >>>

❑ 1. **East Wall Traverse**        *East Wall*        6c
Excellent technical and pumpy work-out. From the jugs on the south wall, traverse low round the *South Arête* to continue under *The Bulge* to drop down to climb the *East Arête*. No high jugs allowed!

❑ 2. **South Arête**        *South Wall*        6c
Sit start south wall undercuts and climb the roofed arête.

❑ 3. **The Bulge**        *East Wall*        4
Climb the centre of the east wall just left of a bulge and surmount it. SS is 6a.

❑ 4. **East Arête**        *East Wall*        4+
Sit start low and match jugs to pinch the arête, lunge to top.

❑ 5. **North Wall**        *North Wall*        4
The north vertical wall through polished holds.

❑ 6. **North Arête**        *North Wall*        4
Sit start at good holds, climb steeply up the undercut arête to jugs.

❑ 7. **North Traverse**        *North Wall*        5
Start on the west side and traverse the handrail left to finish up *North Arête*.

❑ 8. **The Crimps**        *North Wall*        6a
Follow the traverse to use the two crimps on the wall to a tough move up to the top.

❑ 9. **West Arête**        *North Wall*        4+
Follow the traverse for a few moves to climb the arête via a right-hand crimp.

❑ 10. **Clochodrick Traverse** ★  *Girdle*        7a
As for *East Wall Traverse* but continue to a tricky technical section along *North Wall* to drop down and reverse the *North Traverse*.

# ▢ WINDYHILL

WINDYHILL QUARRY

## BLOC NOTES >>>

This pleasant south-facing quarried wall of orange basalt lies on the pleasant 'braes' above Johnstone just west of Paisley. Windyhill is excellent all-year-round, as it faces due south and catches any sun going. It has flat grassy landings, is 5m at its highest, and doesn't suffer from damp. It provides a gradation of traditional straight-up problems from easy to super-eliminate 7a problems. Various traverses can also be contrived. Walk-off descents.

## TRAVEL >>>

| Town | >>> | Elderslie |
|------|-----|-----------|
| Sat Nav | >>> | PA5 0SR |
| Parking | >>> | NS 43429 61390 /// paddle.postage.jetliner |
| Bloc | >>> | NS 43396 61396 /// stew.putts.forwarded |

Just west of Glasgow airport on the M8, take the Irvine exit onto the A737. Exit this at the Kilbarchan junction and head south, turning right at the next roundabout. Head over the railway bridge at Milliken Park and turn left at the next roundabout towards Johnstone. After 1km, turn right at Rannoch Wood entrance and head uphill on Rannoch Road (southwards) for 1km. At the junction at the top of the hill, turn hard left and head north to a carpark (on the right) after 250m. The bouldering quarry is across the road to the west. A bigger quarry sits just north of the carpark in the woods.

## TOP PROBLEMS >>>

❒ 1. **Left Wall Problem 1**                              4
Climb the slabby rib on the far left.

❒ 2. **Left Wall Problem 2**                              4
Climb the vague arête right of the left corner.

❒ 3. **Left Wall 3**                              3
Climb the wall just right again.

❒ 4. **Left Wall 4**                              6a
Sit start the bulging shield feature left of the big easy corner, gaining pinchy sidepulls. Step up and finish more easily.

❒ 5. **Left Wall 5**                              3
Climb the groove left of the easier descent wall left of the big corner.

❒ 6. **Windyhill Wall**                              4
Layback up the shady wall right of the big corner.

❒ 7. **Windyhill Arête**                              5
Bridge up the wee cave niche and climb up the arête on its right, trending right at mid-height on good holds.

❒ 8. **Windyhill Crack ★**                              6a
From the horizontal break, gain the higher crack pockets and finish direct, using holds on the right.

❒ 8a. **Windyhill Crack Eliminate**                              6c
From the horizontal break of the high wall, gain a left-hand sidepull. From this crank straight up on smears to the bottom-most of the three crack pockets and finish direct. Eliminate intermediate holds out right at the start.

❒ 9. **Windyhill Groove**                              4
From the niche right of the wall, climb up and left onto the wall and finish up the hanging groove.

❒ 10. **Niche 1**                              5
Start in the niche but head up directly through an overlap.

❒ 11. **Niche 2**                              4
Climb up right through the overlap.

❒ 12. **Right Wall**                              4
The cracked wall, stepping off a ramp on the right.

❒ 13. **Corner**                              2+
The stepped corner left of *The Bulge*.

❒ 14. **The Bulge**                              6c
Sit start the bulge on the right, gain a sloper, bridge out then surmount the bulge with difficulty trending left. The stand is a bit easier.

❒ 15. **Corner**                              2+
The stepped corner left of *The Bulge*.

❒ 16. **Right Arête**                              3
The fun arête on the right of *The Bulge*.

❒ 17. **The Traverse**                              6c/7a
A low right-to-left traverse along the whole crag. An 'aller-retour' version is 7a.
FA Colin Lambton, 2021.

# ☐ ANDROMEDA STANE

ANDROMEDA STANE

★ The Horn of Andromeda

## BLOC NOTES >>>

A lone but attractive sandstone bloc in the middle of urban Paisley in Charleston Park. A large mat is helpful as landings, whilst grassy, may hold broken glass. It is best visited outside of 'social' hours, so perhaps early mornings are best. Faces due west.

## TRAVEL >>>

| Town | >>> | Paisley |
|------|-----|---------|
| Sat Nav | >>> | PA2 7RG |
| Parking | >>> | NS 48611 62239 /// critic.gloves.player |
| Bloc | >>> | NS 48549 62372 /// values.acid.plus |

The boulder sits in a park between St Charles Primary School and Lochfield Bowling Club, about 1.5km south of Paisley Canal St Railway Station. If driving, gain Lochfield Road in Paisley, then park by the bowling green. Walk north down a small path by the red post box at the side of a small shop. Veer left into the park and at the end of a metal fence turn left to the boulder on a slope overlooking wasteground. First climbed by Joe Kelly and Martin McGlynn in 2019. Problems described right to left.

## TOP PROBLEMS >>>

▢ 1. **Balls of Your Pants Arête**                                  6a
Sit start the overhang on the right of the crack. Pull over the lip onto the face and up the hanging slopey arête.

▢ 2. **The Andromeda Strain** ★                        6c+
Sit start at the base of the crack and travel left on jugs to a tricky sequence to transition into the prow, then finish as for *The Horn of Andromeda*.

▢ 3. **Andromeda's Crack**                                  6a
Sit start under the roof and gain jugs, then climb into the diagonal crack, finish up this, stepping right at the top. The crack on its own is Font 4.

▢ 4. **Nedusa**                                  6a
Sit start left of *Andromeda's Crack*, hands below the graffiti. Gain a left-hand jug, then head right diagonally through *Andromeda's Crack* to finish on a ledge.

▢ 5. **Perseus**                                  6a+
The arête and wall right of the prow and corner. Sit start under the left roof to pull onto ledges and use the arête and wall holds to trend right at the top.

▢ 6. **The Horn of Andromeda** ★                        6c
Sit start the fine wee prow on the left, snapping up to a low double pinch match. Gain a higher left pinch and right crimps, then pull left round the corner to pockets to the top. No left flakes for feet.

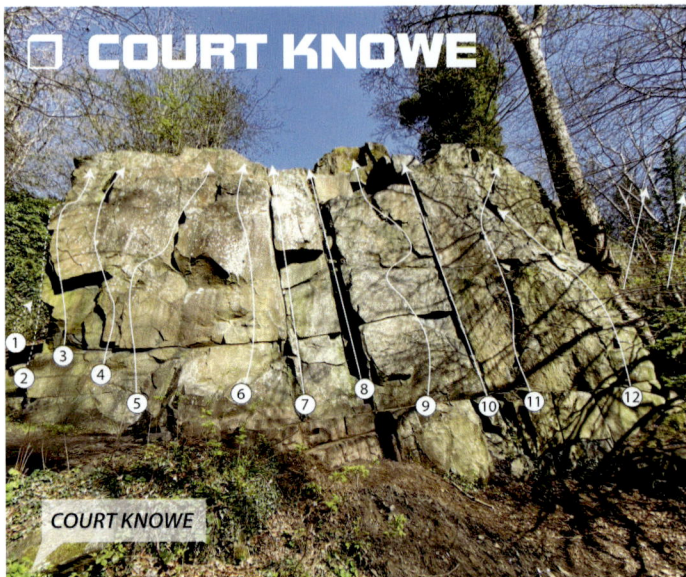

# ❏ COURT KNOWE

COURT KNOWE

## BLOC NOTES >>>

This secluded little quarry in the south side of Glasgow offers some worthwhile problems in a suburban park just oppostie Linn Park. It sits at the top of a hill which Mary Queen of Scots reputedly used as a viewpoint for the Battle of Langside. The quarry's front wall is highball, about 8m at its highest, so the routes are often best top-roped or practised before ascents.

## TRAVEL >>>

| Town | >>> | Cathcart |
|------|-----|----------|
| Sat Nav | >>> | G44 5DX |
| Parking | >>> | NS 58826 59986 /// nation.decks.other |
| Bloc | >>> | NS 58813 60006 /// bowls.retire.poppy |

South Glasgow: Cathcart railway station. Turn left out of the station onto Delvin Road, then left to a bridge over the river to a roundabout. Follow Old Castle Road south past the Old Smiddy pub up the steep hill to steps. Continue over the hill. The quarry sits amongst trees just opposite the entrance to Linn Park.

## TOP PROBLEMS >>>

❏ 1. **There Is No Spoon** ★        *Left Wall*                7a

A solution to the leaning wall on the left side of the quarry. Step off a block by the left crack and gain two thin crimps in a horizontal break, lunge right to match a finger-ledge. From here, gain an edge and a mono, then lunge to jugs at the top. Requires large mats to protect the landing. FA John Watson, 1999.

☐ 2. **Blue Tits Left Hand**     *Front Wall*          5
The arête on the far left, taken from the leaning wall side. Sit start the arête on jugs and layback up to a midway ledge, then the top.

☐ 3. **Blue Tits Right Hand**     *Front Wall*          4+
The left arête up the wee groove and face holds to mantle onto the ledge.

☐ 4. **Wullie's Crack**     *Front Wall*          4+
The left wall via slots to the ledge.

☐ 5. **The Press**     *Front Wall*          4
Take good holds and balance up and right to the wee hanging flake corner.

☐ 6. **DF 118s**     *Front Wall*          6b
The bulge to the right has a chipped pocket. Gain this and dyno for a sloping rail, break left to finish – watch your landing!

☐ 7. **Layback Crack**     *Front Wall*          3+
The cracked corner can be laybacked through the overlap roof.

☐ 8. **Coleoptera Crack**     *Front Wall*          3
The vegetated,wide crack could do with some gardening.

☐ 9. **The Red Pill**     *Front Wall*          7a
Eliminate up the slabby wall. Start via an undercut to a sloping rail, use a hold near the right crack and smear upwards. Pad the plinth landing.

☐ 10. **Thin Fingers Crack**     *Front Wall*          5+
Technical laybacking and smearing up the thin crack, using holds on the left.

☐ 11. **Mountain Climber**     *Front Wall*          3+
Trend right up the highball right wall from *right of 0Thin Fingers Crack*.

☐ 12. **Last Route**     *Front Wall*          3
The right edge climbed beside the tree to trend left at the top.

☐ 13. **Mud Crack**     *Ten Year Wall*          3
Bridge up the crack using both walls to good holds, trend right at the top.

☐ 14. **Ten Year Wall ★**     *Ten Year Wall*          6b
Start centrally, left hand on a ramp press, right on a high right crimp (near but not on a jug). Mantle to the foot ledge and gain the thin central, vertical crimp above. Use poor left crimps to walk feet up and reach direct to the top left jug and mantle. Take care not to fall into the tree stump.

☐ 15. **Ten Year Wall Right**     *Ten Year Wall*          6a
A right variation of the wall, using better holds. Mantle up to the foot ledge, then gain a high right hold, reach left via crimps to bridge out to reach high left to the jug and mantle.

☐ 16. **Consolation**
*Right Wall*          2+
Mantle the ledges on the right to get stood up, then step right.

☐ 17. **Snowy's Big Traverse**     6b
R-L traverse of front face, crux is the *Red Pill* slab section.

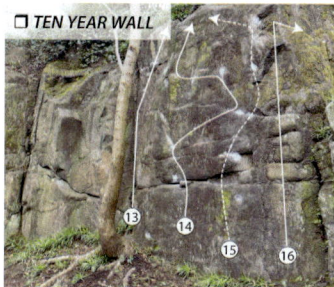
☐ *TEN YEAR WALL*

# ☐ WHITE CART ROOF

★ Lost World

## BLOC NOTES >>>

This small but very steep sandstone wall on the banks of the White Cart Water just north of Busby, was revealed by coal or lignite extraction. It's now an excellent 'pockets' roof which was chipped years ago and abandoned. Despite the artificiality, it has some good roof problems and further link-up projects. The top-out mantles do need a big mat for protection, as the landing drops off awkwardly. It needs very dry conditions and is best with a southerly breeze in summer to rid it of moisture. Don't bother in winter as it is usually too cold and green to dry. Take a big brush to clean up the lips and top-outs.

## TRAVEL >>>

| Town | >>> | Castlemilk |
|---|---|---|
| Sat Nav | >>> | Drakemire Drive G45 9SR |
| Parking | >>> | NS 58748 58604 /// payer.ranged.smile |
| Bloc | >>> | NS 58105 57247 /// agreed.translated.remark |

From the north from the back of Linn Park off Drakemire Drive (park by the cemetery), enter Castlemilk Woodlands. Follow high tracks by the fields due south for 1km to where the old WW2 bunkers appear under the telecom mast. Keep in the woods and follow small trails down towards the river, skirting steep ground to stumble over the caved roof opposite the playing parks at Stamperland. If the river is low, it is better to access from Busby railway station. Go down to the bridge and head north into the park, follow the path under the railway bridge and down to the riverside. 50m north of the Kittoch Water junction and crossing the bloc faces south on the east bank.

## THE PROBLEMS >>>

❑ 1. **La Traversée des Trous 1**          6a
Traverse the lip rightwards from the far left to mantle up to jugs at the niche, rock left onto the slab then step right up the nose on jugs. 4+ from the corner.

❑ 2. **La Traversée des Trous 2**          6b
A little harder: on reaching the corner jugs, finish via *The Nose* problem.

❑ 3. **The Nose**          5+
From the niche corner jugs, pull on and twist up for jugs on the nose, travel right a bit and mantle out onto the nose and top slab.

❑ 4. **Labyrinth**          6c ★
Sit start at a right-hand pocket and poor left sidepull. Slap to the low lip and use the corner sloper only to gain a right-hand pocket on the wall, hook up to lip, trend right and mantle back left on the nose.

❑ 5. **Lost World**          6c+
A stand start at a right-hand undercling pocket and a left-hand pocket. Pull on and boost for the lip and mantle over. A sit start will be much harder.

★ *Rebecca Morris on Utopia*

## BLOC NOTES >>>

A little bit of Fontainebleau in the middle of the city, this collection of nine artificial boulders lies within the River Clyde's 'Cuningar Loop'. Managed by Forestry & Land Scotland, they were created from the 2014 Commonwealth Games legacy fund. The park is part of the Clyde Gateway project and located on reforested land in a loop of the River Clyde east of Dalmarnock and north of Rutherglen. The 'loop' is a pleasant urban activity park of 15 wooded hectares and can be busy at weekends and after school, so early mornings are best for solitude. The boulders are made from sculpted resin concrete, which is generally rough but polished on descents and on some holds. The boulders are skirted with generous gravel traps, so only a small crash mat or doormat is needed to keep the shoes clean. The park has four main areas from beginners to advanced, totalling nine blocs. The biggest single bloc is the overhanging Mammoth Bloc, but the hardest problems lie on the Scratch boulder. It is fun to create circuits of problems to mimic the style of climbing at Fontainebleau.

## TRAVEL >>>

| Town | >>> | Dalmarnock |
|------|-----|------------|
| Sat Nav | >>> | G73 1PW |
| Parking | >>> | NS 62243 62702 /// backup.pinch.yappy |
| Blocs | >>> | NS 62297 63007 /// bride.bits.pace |

Train: from Glasgow Central to Dalmarnock. Go south a little, then turn left along Springfield Road, then follow the signs to Cuningar. A footbridge leads over the Clyde into the park. Turn right (south) for 300m to access the bouldering park.

Car: Come off the M74 at junction 2 and head north-west along the M724 to a second right up Duchess Road, which joins Downiebrae Road and the entrance to the parking is signposted on a corner. A gravel road leads to the parking in 500m. Follow the footpath to the boulder park, which is opposite the bike track.

Bicycle/foot: the park is accessible along the Clyde Cycleway on its north bank. Cross south at Dalmarnock Bridge to Downiebrae Road and follow signs to the park. You can continue along the north bank of the river to the footbridge and walk south through the park to the bouldering.

Notes on boulders: all problems are described initially as stand-up starts. Where the sit start changes the grade or quality of the problems significantly, these are noted as separate problems. Many problems have awkward 'frogging' sit starts due to the lack of undercut walls and do not really benefit from the added difficulty. All problems are described in a clockwise sequence from the descent routes. In the topos, some lines are marked with red and blue lines. These refer to the red and blue circuit problems, topos for these below.

# CUNINGAR BLUE CIRCUIT

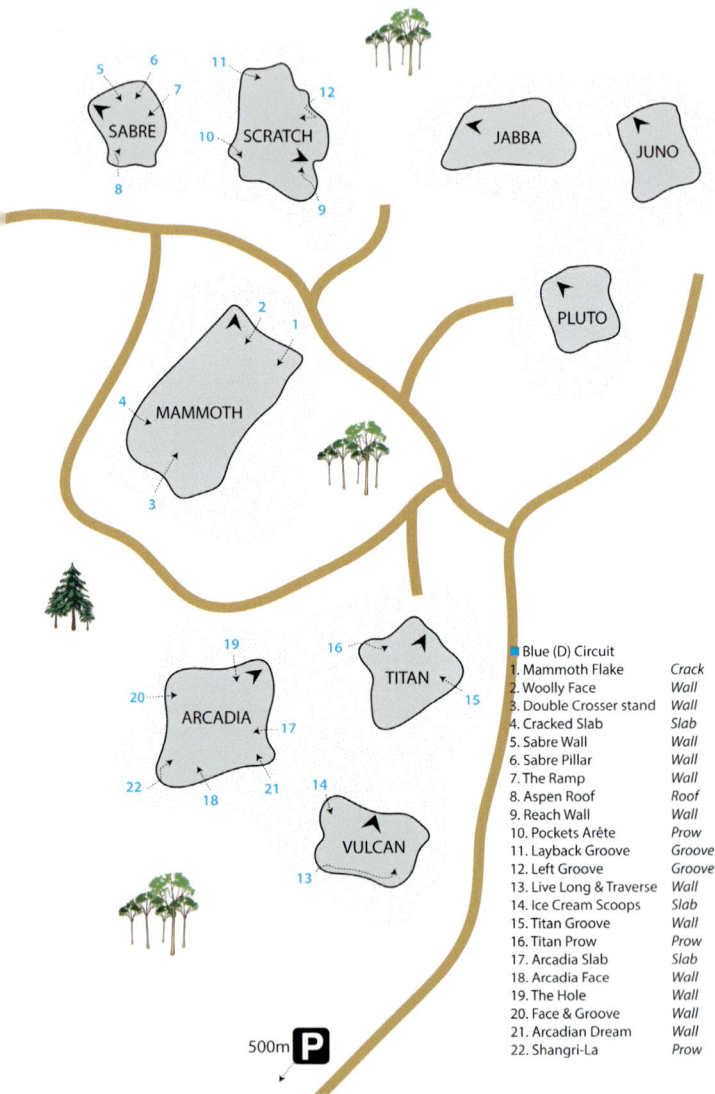

N

SABRE

5
6
7
8

11
SCRATCH
12
10
9

JABBA

JUNO

PLUTO

MAMMOTH

2
1
4
3

TITAN

16
15

ARCADIA

19
20
17
22
18
21

VULCAN

14
13

500m **P**

● Blue (D) Circuit
1. Mammoth Flake — *Crack*
2. Woolly Face — *Wall*
3. Double Crosser stand — *Wall*
4. Cracked Slab — *Slab*
5. Sabre Wall — *Wall*
6. Sabre Pillar — *Wall*
7. The Ramp — *Wall*
8. Aspen Roof — *Roof*
9. Reach Wall — *Wall*
10. Pockets Arête — *Prow*
11. Layback Groove — *Groove*
12. Left Groove — *Groove*
13. Live Long & Traverse — *Wall*
14. Ice Cream Scoops — *Slab*
15. Titan Groove — *Wall*
16. Titan Prow — *Prow*
17. Arcadia Slab — *Slab*
18. Arcadia Face — *Wall*
19. The Hole — *Wall*
20. Face & Groove — *Wall*
21. Arcadian Dream — *Wall*
22. Shangri-La — *Prow*

# ♀ CUNINGAR RED CIRCUIT

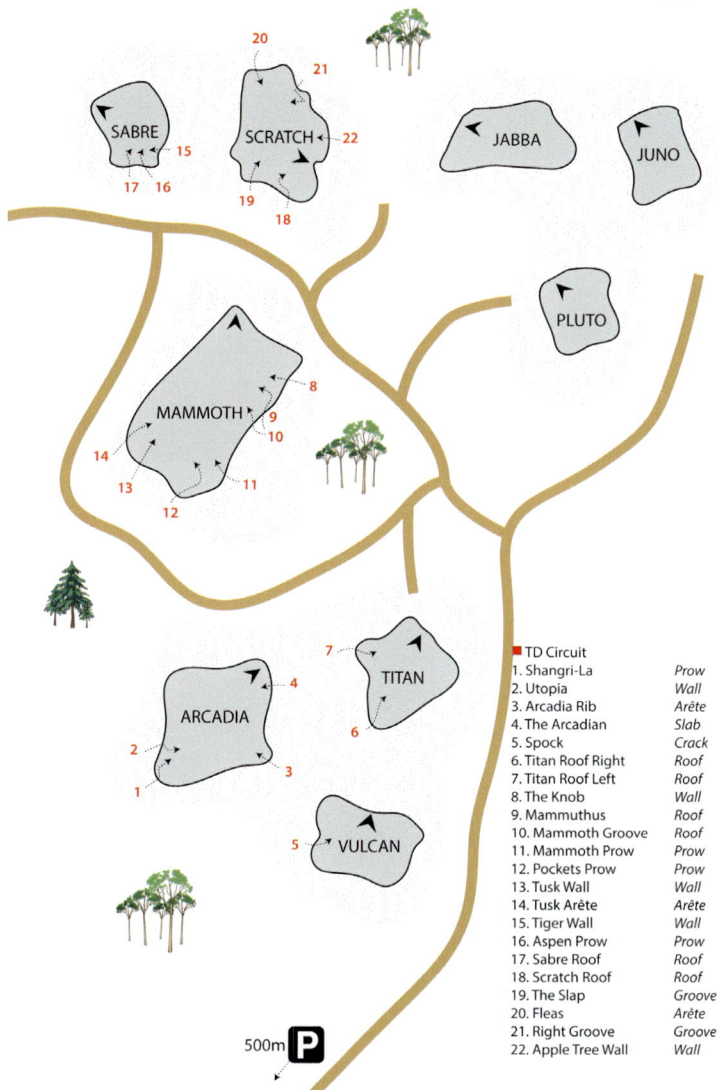

**N**

SABRE

20
21
SCRATCH ← 22
15
17  16
19
18

JABBA

JUNO

PLUTO

MAMMOTH
8
9
10
14
13
11
12

TITAN
7
4
6

ARCADIA
2
1
3

VULCAN
5

■ TD Circuit

| | |
|---|---|
| 1. Shangri-La | *Prow* |
| 2. Utopia | *Wall* |
| 3. Arcadia Rib | *Arête* |
| 4. The Arcadian | *Slab* |
| 5. Spock | *Crack* |
| 6. Titan Roof Right | *Roof* |
| 7. Titan Roof Left | *Roof* |
| 8. The Knob | *Wall* |
| 9. Mammuthus | *Roof* |
| 10. Mammoth Groove | *Roof* |
| 11. Mammoth Prow | *Prow* |
| 12. Pockets Prow | *Prow* |
| 13. Tusk Wall | *Wall* |
| 14. Tusk Arête | *Arête* |
| 15. Tiger Wall | *Wall* |
| 16. Aspen Prow | *Prow* |
| 17. Sabre Roof | *Roof* |
| 18. Scratch Roof | *Roof* |
| 19. The Slap | *Groove* |
| 20. Fleas | *Arête* |
| 21. Right Groove | *Groove* |
| 22. Apple Tree Wall | *Wall* |

500m P

JABBA SOUTH & EAST

JUNO NORTH

## JABBA

The long low slabby boulder, the westernmost of the three introductory boulders.

❑ 1. **Easy Arête** 2
Descent route up the sloping south arête.
❑ 2. **Left Eye** 2
Up the central south slab through an eye feature.
❑ 3. **Right Eye** 2
Up the right on the southern slab.
❑ 4. **Slabby Arête** 2
Up the slabby eastern arête.
❑ 5. **Pocket Face** 2
Up the slabby eastern pocketed face.
❑ 6. **Pocket Face Hands Free** 3
The north slab facing the trees. Hands free using feet and knees only.
❑ 7. **Jabba's Crack** 2+
Up the runnel crack on the north side.
❑ 8. **Max Rebo** 2+
Climb the bulging slab right of *Jabba's Crack*.
❑ 9. **Jabba Girdle** 3
From the descent, girdle rightwards (anticlockwise) around the boulder. Time your traverse and try and beat your record to standing on the descent ledge.

## JUNO

The middlemost of the three introductory boulders.
❑ 1. **Juno Arête** 2
The sloping west arête is also the descent.
❑ 2. **Juno North Face** 3
Climb the central north face.
❑ 3. **Juno Pockets** 3
Climb the northeast pocketed face to a rounded mantle.
❑ 4. **Juno Face** 3+
Climb the steeper southern face through the overlap.
❑ 5. **Juno Groove** 3
Climb the runnel groove on the right of the descent face.
❑ 6. **Juno Girdle** 5
From the descent, climb around the boulder clockwise.

PLUTO NORTH

VULCAN SOUTH

VULCAN NORTH

## PLUTO

The southmost boulder of the three introductory level boulders.

❑ 1. **Donald Face**                                                  2

Climb the scooped centre of the east face. Also a descent.

❑ 2. **East Arête**                                                    2+

The steep east arête is turned on the right at the top.

❑ 3. **Goofy Face**                                                    3

Climb the centre of the southeast face.

❑ 4. **South Arête**                                                   2+

The short but steep arête is turned on the left at the top.

❑ 5. **Pluto Groove**                                                  2+

The short scoop and groove in the centre of the west face.

❑ 6. **Pluto Descent Arête**                                           2

The western slabby arête is also a good descent.

❑ 7. **Pluto Arête**                                                   2

The north arête right of *Donald Face*.


## VULCAN

The southernmost boulder in a cluster of three, the first on the approach from the south past the bike track.

❑ 1. **Vulcan Face**                                                   2

The north scoop is also the descent.

❑ 2. **Vulcan Arête**                                                  4+

Climb the blunt arête left of the descent to a tricky mantle topout.

❑ 3. **Vulcan Death Grip**                                             4

Climb the left side of the arête with tricky moves.

❑ 4. **Troddle**                                                       3+

Undercut the southeast wall up to good holds and mantle the top.

❑ 5. **Vulcan Centre**                                                 3

Climb the central section of the south wall to the scooped finish.

❑ 6. **Live Long and Traverse**                                        4+

Traverse L-R along the south face on good holds to finish above *Troddle*.

❑ 7. **Live Long and Prosper**                                         4

The left side of the south wall through the curving ramp.

❑ 8. **Live Long and Girdle**                                          6b

Girdle traverse anticlockwise (right) from the descent.

❑ 9. **Vulcan Groove**                                                 5

Climb the wide western groove crack to a tricky top on poor footholds.

❑ 10. **Spock** ★                                                      5

Climb the blunt rib left of the wider crack to mantle direct via slopey ramp.

❑ 11. **The Ice Cream Scoop**                                          4

Step into a foot scoop and gain slopers above to mantle out left.

❑ 12. **Vulcan Sign**                                                  5

From the descent ledge step right into the foot scoop and finish direct through slopers.

ARCADIA SOUTH & EAST

ARCADIA NORTH & WEST

## ARCADIA

❑ 1. **Descent Route**                                          2
The stepped but high northern arête is also the descent.

❑ 2. **The Arcadian** ★                                      6a
The right side of the slab direct all the way with no recourse to the descent.

❑ 3. **Arcadia Slab** ★                                       4+
The slab and shield on the left of the slab, then smear up slopers to mantle.

❑ 4. **Arcadia Rib**                                          6a+
The rib direct between the slab and the groove is thin and hard.

❑ 5. **Arcadian Dream**                                       5+
The southern grooved slot is bridged to the top via a mantle.

❑ 6. **Arcadia Hard Face**                                    5
Climb the face direct just left of the groove, using holds in the groove and face.

❑ 7. **Arcadia Face**                                         4+
The southern wall through the patina shield crimps to a juggy ramp to the top.

❑ 8. **Shangri-La** ★                                        5+
The excellent southwest prow moving left round the prow at the top.

❑ 9. **Utopia**                                               5+
The right side of the wall, between the scoop and the prow, taken direct.

❑ 10. **Face and Groove**                                     4+
Climb the wee rib on the west face to pull left into the top hanging groove.

❑ 11. **Et In Arcadia Ego**                                   5
Stand on the ramp on the west arête and climb direct to the top.

❑ 12. **Leap of Faith**                                       5
Start in the middle of the face, gain the juggy sidepulls to a direct finish.

❑ 13. **The Hole**                                            4+
Climb into the hole to better holds, finish direct, or go right up the west arête.

★ *Tipteoing up Arcadia Slab*

TITAN SOUTH & EAST

TITAN NORTH & WEST

## TITAN

❑ 1. **Titan's Ladder**                    2
The northern stepped arête. Also the descent.

❑ 2. **Lunar Face**                         4
The eastern face is crimpy.

❑ 3. **Titan Groove**                       4+
A technical rib and groove on the east side of the boulder.

❑ 4. **Titan Face**                         3
The pocketed vertical wall on the eastern side of the boulder, right of the roof.

❑ 5. **Titan Roof Right** ★                 6a
The right side of the roof from good holds to a hidden jug, then mantle!

❑ 6. **Titan Roof Direct**                  6a+
The central roof from the undercut direct up over the lip, no jugs left or right.

❑ 7. **Titan Roof Left**                    6a+
The left roof. Gain a good jug on the roof lip and pull over using slopey holds.

❑ 8. **Titan Prow** ★                       5+
Start under the left roof at a sidepull jug on the prow and reach up to a good right jug. A high left toe allows a reach to holds on the left wall flake to top.

❑ 9. **Titan Face**                         5
The northern wall right of the descent, through crimps to a long reach to top.

❑ 10. **Titan Girdle**                      6b
Full clockwise girdle of the Titan boulder from the descent.

★ *Titan Prow*

MAMMOTH SOUTH & EAST

MAMMOTH SOUTH

**MAMMOTH**

☐ 1. **Descent Route** 2

The descent. The stepped arête on the north side of the boulder.

☐ 2. **Green Wall** 3

The wall just left of the descent.

☐ 3. **Woolly Face** 4

The left wall through the ramp and crimps to a sloper topout.

☐ 4. **Mammoth Flake** 4

The excellent cracked arête, taken as layaways on its left side to a direct mantle finish at the top.

☐ 5. **Volx Traverse** 6c

Sit start *Mammoth Flake* at pockets. Traverse low left on pockets and sidepulls to a tricky crossover sequence to gain the big holds in *Mammoth Groove*. Drop down left to undercuts on the left of *Ivory Ramp* and down to a jug. Continue up *Volx* through a crux sequence to finish on the south wall via *Double Crosser*.

☐ 5a. **Volx Traverse Ext. 1** 6c+

Finish up *Tusk Wall* instead.

☐ 5b. **Volx Traverse Ext. 2** 7a

Finish across *Tusk Wall* and into *Tusk Arête*, turning it on the low left.

☐ 6. **The Knob** 6a

Crouch start underclinging the knob feature and gain slopers above, then lunge up and right for a jug, finish direct more easily.

☐ 7. **Mammuthus** 6a

Sit start in the *Mammoth Groove* pockets and gain twin crimps up and right, then a high right-hand sloper to gain jugs to finish.

☐ 8. **Mammoth Groove** 6a

Sit start at pockets and gain large undercuts in the groove, step high and gain a big pocket, match and slap left for a jug, then mantle out the hanging groove. The stand is the same grade.

☐ 8a. **Mammoth Groove Right** 6b

*The Knob* but from slopers go left on higher pockets to gain *Mammoth Groove*.

☐ 9. **Ivory Ramp** 6b

Sit start the overhanging rib/ramp feature. Using undercuts, gain higher jugs and finish via *Mammoth Prow*.

☐ 9a. **Ivory Superdirect** 6c+

Eliminate. *Ivory Ramp Sit Start* to the big right central sloper, then a long move to a crimp under the lip, then jump up right to jug and over the top.

☐ 9b. **Cuningar Leap ★** 7a

Sit start *Pockets Roof* but traverse at head-height under the roof rightwards to join the dynamic crux of *Ivory Superdirect*.

☐ 10. **Mammoth Prow** 6a

Stand-up. Use all big holds on the prow over the lip to the dishes at the top.

☐ 11. **Volx** 6b

Sit start at a jug and press up left through a pocket to edges and finish left round the corner into *Double Crosser*. A more direct version is 6b+.

MAMMOTH WEST

★ Harry Leitch on Green River

❒ 12. **Pockets Roof**                                            6a+

Sit start at a finger jug and climb up right on pockets, then take a crux pull left through the roof on slopey edges. A right finish through the roof is harder.

❒ 13. **Double Crosser** ★                                        5

Takes the narrow wall just left of the prow, from a good finger ledge. Involves various crossover moves up the high slopers to the top (a sit start is 5+).

❒ 14. **Tusk Wall**                                               6a

Takes the wall just right of the arête. Sidepulls allow higher holds to be gained and a step right at the top. No jugs out right.

❒ 15. **Tusk Arête** ★                                            6a+

Take the blunt arête direct, using a high sloper on the right and a crimp sidepull on the left slab. Step up the higher arête using crimps near the top.

❒ 16. **Cracked Slab**                                            4+

The cracked slab and high scoop just left of the blank *Tusk Arête*.

❒ 17. **Green River**                                             4

Climb the river-like cracks just right of the patinas, stepping left at the top.

❒ 18. **Megafauna Patinas**                                       3+

Climb the concrete shields on sharp edges to mantle the top.

❒ 19. **Megafauna Traverse**                                      4+

Traverse rightwards from the descent to finish up and into the *Cracked Slab*.

❒ 20. **Mammoth Girdle** ★                                        7a

Technical. From the descent, traverse anti-clockwise round *Tusk Arête,* then low along the overhanging front wall to turn *Mammoth Flake* back to the descent.

★ *Harry Leitch on Mammoth Prow*

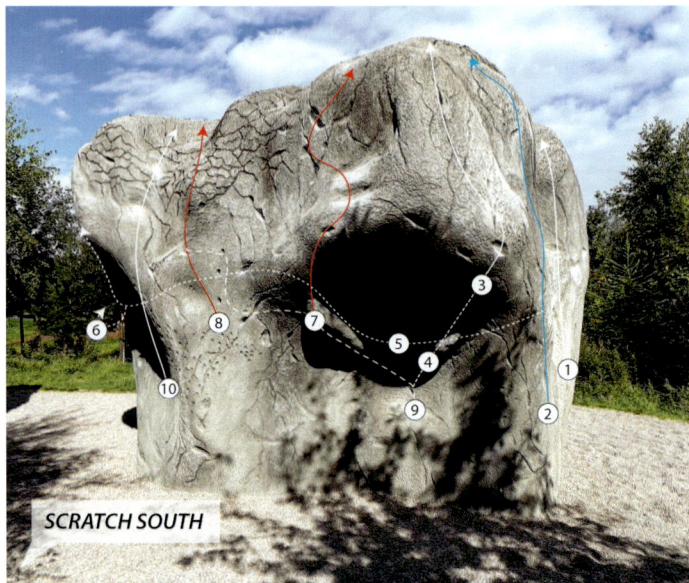

SCRATCH SOUTH

SCRATCH WEST & SOUTH

## SCRATCH

☐ 1. **Scratch Groove**                                        3

The descent. The groove on the southeast side is a balancy ascent which is also tricky to descend.

☐ 2. **Reach Wall**                                        5

Climb the wall left of the descent route, next to the prow. A long right-hand reach sorts this one out. Step left at the top.

☐ 3. **Scratch Prow**                                    6a

Stand start at the right side of the roof, with holds on each side of the prow. Bearhug up this to a step right at the top.

☐ 4. **Psoriasis**                                    6b

Sit start to *Scratch Prow* from under the roof on holds on the right-hand undercut. Gain the prow to finish as for the stand-up.

☐ 5. **Psoriasis Roof Traverse**                    6b+

Pull on at descent route and traverse clockwise under the roof to eventually join *Dermatitis* and finish up *Pockets Arête*.

☐ 6. **Dermatology**                                    6c

Traverse clockwise from the descent route through *Psoriasis Roof*, keeping low through *Dermatitis / Pockets Arête* (no holds on the bulge overhead). Continue along *Pockets Wall* to eventually finish up *Layback Groove* onto the top of *Fleas*.

☐ 7. **Scratch Roof** ★                                6a

An excellent roof problem. Stand start at the twin undercuts in the roof and reach up right to slopers. Pull through the roof and use a left-hand hold to slap for a hidden sloper on the lip. Mantle out.

☐ 7a. **Flakey**                                    6b

Sit start from the right undercut hold to left undercuts then into *Scratch Roof*.

☐ 8. **The Slap**                                    6a

Stand start just left of the roof at edges and make a slap move to a high sloper over a bulge, match, then mantle left into the hanging groove.

☐ 9. **The Pox**                                    6c

Eliminate but good. Sit start the left undercuts to a low left crimp, then cross to the top of three monos, gain a left crimp and finish as for *The Slap*.

☐ 10. **Eczema**                                    6a+

Stand start at edges on the right of the vague arête of the scoop, gain slopers and finish up and right into the hanging groove.

☐ 11. **The Scoop** ★                                6a

Stand into the scoop and press left to holds on *Pockets Arête* and up.

☐ 12. **Dermatitis**                                    6b

Sit start on pockets under *Eczema* in the scoop, get stood up then make a technical leftward sequence to gain *Pockets Arête* and finish up this.

☐ 13. **Pockets Arête**                                4+

Climb the arête from the left into pockets to trend right at the top to a mantle. SS 6a.

☐ 14. **Pockets Wall**                                5+

Climb the central pocketed wall to a direct mantle. SS is 6a.

SCRATCH NORTH & EAST

★ Harry Nicholson on Pox

❒ 15. **Pockets Wall Left**                              6a
A harder version between the centre and *Layback Groove*, to rejoin the central mantle at the top.

❒ 16. **Layback Groove**                              5
Layback up the north-west groove via slopers and good edges to mantle out left onto the top of *Fleas Arête*.

❒ 17. **Fleas Arête**                              6a
Stand start the north bulge using holds on the right bulge arête and gain the right sloper, then mantle up direct.

❒ 18. **Fleas Arête Crouch**                              6b
Crouch start the blunt bulge and use compression moves and heels to gain the stand-up.

❒ 19. **Fleas ★**                              6b+
Crouch start *Fleas Arête* but gain the left sloper on the wall and kick left on the groove then use slopers to climb direct to the top.

❒ 20. **Right Groove**                              6a
Use a left undercut in the groove to jump up right to a sloper on the wall, then squirm up the groove a little to gain higher slopers and finish direct.

❒ 21. **Itchy & Scratchy Show**                              6c
Crouch start the central rib between the two grooves, at about waist-height, and gain the good finger jugs then up *Right Groove*.

❒ 22. **Left Groove**                              5
From good edges on the rib, bridge up the groove to finish direct through slopers. A left finish is also possible at the top at the same grade.

❒ 23. **RTFM**                              6a
A sit start to *Left Groove*. From sidepull slopers pull on and use a right heel to make a tough move round the rib to the blind edges, then finish direct.

❒ 24. **Apple Tree Bulge**                              5+
The right side of the leaning wall by *Left Groove*. Use heels to gain high edges and finish direct.

❒ 24a. **Apple Tree Bulge Sit**                              6b
Sit start the left groove and transition into the stand-up.

❒ 25. **Apple Tree Wall ★**                              6a
The leaning wall just right of the descent route, taken direct. Use sidepulls to pull on and climb straight up the wall to a technical section at half-height, finish over the bulge via slopey edges. A sit start from holds on the left or in the groove on the right makes it 6b either way.

❒ 26. **Hard Apples ★**                              7a
A good technical traverse. Crouch start *Fleas* to the flat left dish hold, match this, then undercut out left through *Right Groove* to cross into its good holds, drop down with hard moves into the base of *Left Groove*, then transition left into the stand-up of *Apple Tree Wall* (crux).

SABRE EAST

SABRE SOUTH

**SABRE**

❑ 1. **Rapier**                                         2
The ramp line on the north-west wall. Climb up left on good holds into a scooped finish. Also the descent route.

❑ 2. **Rapier Direct**                                 3
Climb the wall just left of the descent ramp, using slopers on the descent and holds on the face, mantle right at the top.

❑ 3. **Sabre Wall**                                    5
The slabby wall left of the descent route. Start on the good hold on the left arête and trend up right with a long reach to better holds in the scoop.

❑ 4. **Sabre Pillar**                                 4+
Take the pillar-like arête direct from a shield feature via a right-hand sloper and good left-hand incut, mantle the top.

❑ 5. **Sabre Face**                                    4
Start on the shield feature as for *Sabre Pillar*, but travel left and up on good holds to mantle the face just left of the pillar finish.

❑ 6. **Sabre Slopers**                                5+
Match the sloper at the base of the ramp, match a high right sloper and gain more slopers over the top. Eliminate incuts out right.

❑ 7. **The Ramp**                                      4
Stand start with hands on the ramp and pull up onto this and climb through it via slopers to the top.

❑ 8. **Funfest**                                       5+
Crouch start from a left-hand sidepull/undercling and a right-hand crimp under the slopey rail of *The Ramp*. Gain the rail and ride it to the top straight up.

❑ 9. **Tiger**                                        6a+
Climb the wall left of the ramp direct via edges and pockets (right hand not allowed on ramp holds). Tricky feet allow a high left hold to be gained then a right sloper. Finish directly to the top.

❑ 10. **Aspen Prow**                                  5+
Stand start the handrail jug on the right side of the southern roof. Pull on and climb through the roof/prow and slightly right to a good pinch/sidepull hold, then finish directly via a mantle.

❑ 11. **Sabre Roof**                                   6a
The central, south roof. Crouch start at a large undercling and gain the handrail. Climb directly through a shield feature with opposing sidepulls to mantle out direct.

❑ 12. **Aspen Roof**                                  5+
The left side of the roof from a stand-start. From good sidepulls on the flake pull up to a jug above the hand rail, heel-hook and reach up left on the wall to an edge. Pull over the roof and finish up the short wall with a mantle.

❑ 13. **To the Hilt**                                 6a+
Sit start the flake and travel up right through the hand rail to join *Sabre Roof*.

❑ 14. **Short Wall**                                  4+
Climb the wall just right of the descent to a rounded mantle.

GLASGOW
**THE NEWSROOM**

## 2 GLASGOW CENTRES | 1 MEMBERSHIP

**THE NEWSROOM IS A WELCOMING BOULDERING CENTRE IN KINNING PARK** | CAFE | COURSES + COACHING | KIDS CLIMBING AREA | SHOP | COMPS | TRAINING FACILITIES | FREE ON-STREET PARKING

**THECLIMBINGACADEMY.COM**

THE CLIMBING ACADEMY

★ *Koon Morris on Dumby's Shattered Low Traverse © Roxanna Barry*